IT'S TIME

ONE HUNDRED AND ONE WAYS TO CHANGE YOUR LIFE

By Best-Selling Author
DIANNE WILSON

My Life's Purpose ...
To know Jesus and to make Him known.

The Author

Dianne is a bestselling author and spokesperson on the issues of body+soul+spirit, healthy living, healthy body image, value and identity. Dianne alongside her husband Jonathan, are the Senior Pastors of Newport Church in Orange County, California. Dianne's entrepreneurial approach to life, and her passionate message of freedom have created a platform for her to help many people. Her insight, wisdom and commitment have resulted in many people understanding their true value. Dianne has devoted her life to this cause — seeing people live in freedom and released into all that they were created to be, body+soul+spirit. Born and raised in Sydney, Australia, wife of an amazing husband, mother of many gorgeous children, and grandmother too, Dianne is a passionate church builder - loving God, loving people and loving life!

Other Books by Dianne Wilson:

- ★ Body & Soul
- ★ Here To Eternity
- ★ Fat Free Forever!
- ★ Back in Shape After Baby
- ★ Fat Free Forever Cookbook
- ★ Fat Free Forever 101 Tips
- ★ Easy Exercise for Everybody

Lifestyle Courses by Dianne Wilson:

- ★ Mirror Mirror
- ★ Body & Soul

IT'S TIME Published by Dianne Wilson

First published in the USA in 2011

ISBN 978-0-9840-3871-8

Photography of Dianne Wilson: Natalie Chenier

www.natalielynnphotography.com

Cover Graphics: Corey Meyers

Typeset in Newport Beach California Printed in the USA

Author Contact Details:

Dianne Wilson

Newport Church PO Box 9577

Newport Beach, CA 92667 USA

Email: dianne.wilson@newportchurch.com

Tel: +1.949.706.2812

Dear God,
Thank you for the privilege of knowing Jesus and making Him known.
Amen.

CONTENTS

Introduction

My life's purpose is to know Jesus and to make Him known. I often think about Jesus and His three years of public ministry and about all that he achieved in the short time He lived here on earth. I think about His relationship with His Heavenly Father and I think about His love and devotion towards people – all people. I also think about His relationship with his team – the disciples.

> "Jesus also did many other things. If they were all written down, I suppose the whole world could not contain the books that would be written."
> [John 21:25 NLT]

When my husband Jonathan and I started our church – Newport Church – in July 2006 we were incredibly excited about the potential of building something from nothing. We were entrusted with a group of graduating Bible College students from Hillsong International Leadership College. These young American students were keen like us to build something from scratch. This group of individuals became our team and most are still with us in Newport Beach, California today. We thank God every day for the privilege we have of serving Him, of building His church, of loving people and loving life in ministry. There is no greater place to be than knowing you are in the right place at the right time with the right people doing the right thing. We are truly grateful. Within a short period of time – just a few months – it became evident to Jonathan and I that this incredibly gifted team of individuals needed us to help them develop new life skills as they transitioned from college life to the real world.

The real world is where work is not optional and paying bills on time is not negotiable. The real world is where healthy relationships actually have to move from chemistry to construction. The real world is where church planting from scratch means setting up and packing down three times every Sunday in three different locations, and still going strong five years on!

At times Jonathan and I have moved between 'Pastoring' and 'Parenting' our young team, as we have tried to help them negotiate life, the universe, and all that is involved in building a significant church for the glory of God. We love our team dearly and appreciate each and every one of them greatly. We admire the strength and integrity of those who have, and continue to lay down their lives, Romans 12 style.

I am beyond grateful to have been raised in a healthy home with wonderful parents [who still are madly deeply in love 50 years on] and I'm beyond grateful to have been led by such amazing leaders, Pastors Brian and Bobbie Houston at Hillsong Church in Sydney, Australia. Not everyone has the privilege of amazing parents or amazing pastors but every Christian has the privilege of knowing Jesus and making Him known. Regardless of background or experience, we are committed to our team – to lead them to Jesus so they can lead Him to others.

The average age of our team when we started was 23. No-one had any experience in church planting but everyone was ready and raring to go. If we could choose our team all over again, we would choose passionate energy and enthusiasm over experience any day. The advantages of youth are obvious: high energy, zealousness, adventurous, risk takers. We love the energy of our team and will be forever grateful that God has entrusted Newport Church to our care.

It was December 2006 when I had come to realize that the initial 'honeymoon' period was somewhat over for some of our team – especially the girls. I could see what was happening; they had begun to 'do' ministry as though it was 'industry', and this led me to coin the phrase 'the industry of ministry' – something that we have worked and continue to work at eliminating in our leadership team.

It is all too easy to go through the motions serving God and allowing oneself to become disconnected from a true and life-giving relationship with Jesus, with the Word of God and with the family of God in which He has placed you. We all need more Jesus every day, and those who are called to serve Him in a full-time capacity can't survive without that life-giving connection.

I went to sleep one evening and realized that 'someone needed to do something' about the way that the girls on the team had started to become familiar with each other and then form circles of connection with some and not others. I played the movie out in my mind and realized that if someone didn't do something soon to help strengthen the back bone of these young women, then slowly but surely they would be picked off by the enemy, under the guise of 'helpful' voices telling them to 'find balance', to 'pull back', to 'rest easy'. These amazing young women didn't join us on this adventure so that someone could come alongside them and give them an excuse to 'check out'.

I went to sleep realizing what needed to happen and awoke the next morning realizing that 'someone' would need to be me. There are always well-meaning people in church life who love to come alongside people and give them advice. The only problem is that those people usually aren't the ones who have signed up for the big life. We need to encourage people – especially young people – that the big God life is the best God life to live!

"A team needs to be constantly rejuvenated by the infusion of young blood. It needs young people with the imagination and the guts to turn everything upside down if they can. It also needs old fogies to keep them from turning upside down those things that ought to be right side up. Above all, it needs young rebels and old conservatives who can work together, challenge each other's values, yield or hold fast with equal grace, and continue after each hard-fought battle to respect each other."
Together We Can [the book compiled by Dan Zadra ©2006 Compendium Incorporated]

Well meaning but unenlightened people usually aren't the role models that young men and women want to lay down their lives for and serve. People who offer advice of more 'balance' without revelation that the Kingdom of God is wonderfully all-consuming, don't help anyone. Balance is not one extreme or another. Balance is the tension found between the two, within any chosen lifestyle. When we choose Kingdom first, then we can find perfect balance within that choice. Be aware of anyone who offers advice that could take you out of the white-hot center of the wonderful action and activity that exists building the Kingdom of God.

I decided to start Chicktime to help our young women understand that they had already made one of the finest decisions of their life by seeking God's Kingdom first. Chicktime is a leadership ministry in our church that is by invitation only, for those who want to grow in ministry. It is specifically designed to help build character; character development that helps individuals flourish and stay at their post, unswervingly. Kingdom first isn't family second and job third.

The Kingdom first lifestyle is clearly described in the Bible; it's Jesus at the center of every aspect of our life. We need to have a revelation that there is balance and every other thing we need found within the Kingdom first life.

> "But seek (aim at and strive after) first of all His kingdom and His righteousness (His way of doing and being right), and then all these things taken together will be given you besides."
> [Matthew 6:33 AMP]

Jesus didn't come to earth to celebrate the disciples' gifts. Jesus came to earth to challenge human hearts to the core. Heart is everything, capacity grows and every good gift comes from God anyway! It's what we do with our gift that is of greatest importance to God.

My husband Jonathan describes our leadership selection criteria very simply, in the following order of importance:

LEADERSHIP SELECTION CRITERIA:

1. HEART
2. CAPACITY
3. GIFT

[In that order.]

The refining of the human heart is an interesting process. Some people have a 'bring it on' spirit and want to change and grow, and others fear the refining process because they are too attached to their dysfunctional life. Sadly dysfunction can be addictive in some people's lives.

Change is essential if we want to fulfill the call of God on our lives. The refining of the heart and the renewing of the mind makes a way for us to change for good.

As leaders, if we don't choose to change then change will happen that we cannot choose. The Kingdom of God will continue to advance and overtake those who choose to stubbornly stand in the way. We need to lead, follow, or we need to move out of the way!

Let's be committed to change for good! As Pastor Brian Houston says, "Life is short and life is long." Let's remember that we have one life and it lasts just a moment. It is also long enough for us to make it count. Let's make it count – for time and eternity. The cover of this book depicts time and eternity: an hourglass at half time and the Bible in a Year – a little tattered and worn.

I gave the Bible in a Year as a Christmas gift to all of the Chicktime girls a couple of years ago. The tattered and worn Bible on the front of this book belongs to one of the young women. She has read it ever since and her life is forever changed and continues to change every single day.

Let's make life count. Where will you be in five years time? 260 weeks time? 1825 days time? 2,333,000 minutes time? If we want a preferred future, we need to plan now, change now, live now.

> "Don't say you don't have enough time. You have exactly the same number of hours per day that were given to Helen Keller, Louis Pasteur, Michelangelo, Mother Teresa, Leonardo da Vinci, Thomas Jefferson and Albert Einstein."
>
> - H. Jackson Brown, Jr.

This book is a collection of outlines and messages and scriptures that I have shared with our team over the last five years. I pray it helps you as much as it has helped, and continues to help us, know Jesus and to make Him known.

IT'S TIME!

Why We Love Chicktime

[memoirs of chicktime]

1. Accountability.

2. Expectancy.

3. Leadership training.

4. Vulnerability [someone always cries – good tears].

5. Destiny friendships outside my social circle.

6. Opportunity.

7. Truth and grace.

8. Kingdom balance with take home value.

9. Relevance.

10. Purpose.

THE 'AND' LIFE

"The master in the art of living makes little distinction between his work and his play, his labor and his leisure, his mind and his body, his information and his recreation, his love and his religion. He hardly knows which is which. He simply pursues his vision of excellence at whatever he does, leaving others to decide whether he is working or playing. To him he's always doing both." - James A. Michener

"Lead, follow, or get out of the way."

- Thomas Paine

A Good Recovery

There is a process for us to be able to 'recover' or start again every time we blow it. We have been saved by grace so that process doesn't include our own good works. It does however require us to acknowledge what we have done and to take appropriate action to make the wrong right again. There is a difference between regret, remorse and repentance. And the road to recovery is found when we dig deep and move beyond regret and remorse, into true repentance.

1. Regret

   Regret describes emotions ranging from being disappointed to intense sorrow due mainly to an external circumstance or event. An example is: we regret that the turkey sandwiches have run out. We can also regret a wrong done, as in: we regret a mistake we've made. Regret is like the sad song of our heart playing on repeat – playing time and time again.

2. Remorse

   Remorse describes deep regret, involving anguish or guilt and self-reproach. Remorse is felt by someone for a wrong they have committed. Perhaps we felt remorse for lying to a leader. Remorse is from the Latin word 'remordere' meaning, 'to bite again'. Remorse is a gnawing feeling of guilt from a past wrong. Regret is from the French word 'regreter/regrater' and originally was a synonym for 'regrate' meaning 'complaint, lament'. Remorse always bites again.

3. Repentance

   There are three Greek words used in the New Testament to denote repentance:

   i. The verb 'metamelomai' is used of a change of mind, such as to produce regret or even remorse on account of sin, but not necessarily a change of heart. This word is used with reference to the repentance of Judas in Matthew 27:3.
   ii. 'Metanoeo', meaning to change one's mind and purpose, as the result of after knowledge.
   iii. This verb 'metanoeo', with the cognate noun 'metanoia', is used of true repentance, a change of mind and purpose and life, to which remission of sin is promised.

   Evangelical repentance consists of:

   i. a true sense of one's own guilt and sinfulness;
   ii. an apprehension of God's mercy in Christ;
   iii. an actual hatred of sin and turning from it to God;
   iv. a persistent endeavor after a holy life in a walking with God in the way of his commandments.

   But repentance comprehends not only such a sense of sin, but also an apprehension of mercy, without which there can be no true repentance.

   (Reference: Easton's 1897 Bible Dictionary)

We need to choose not to live in regret or remorse but to allow God's way of repentance to give us the brand new start we really need and want.

> "Guard your heart above all else, for it determines the course of your life."
> [Proverbs 4:23 NLT]

A Two Way Street

I can remember driving down a narrow road one morning when all of a sudden a car flew around the corner and started to drive toward me. They stopped just in front of me, leaving little room for either of us to move. I sat there wondering what on earth this person was doing driving in the middle of the road, until I realized I was driving in the wrong direction.

Sometimes life can be like that - where we forget that we aren't the only driver on the road and that we need to share and that sometimes it may be us going in the wrong direction. Leadership is a two way street with plenty of room to lead and to follow and to negotiate this adventure called life.

Do your followers admire your leadership?

> "Whatever Saul gave David to do, he did it—and did it well. So well that Saul put him in charge of his military operations. Everybody, both the people in general and Saul's servants, approved of and admired David's leadership."
> [1 Samuel 18:5 The Message]

Remember, leadership is a two way street! It is not all about me and it's not all about you. It's all about us working together.

> "The mark of a good leader is loyal followers; leadership is nothing without a following..."
> [Proverbs 14:28 The Message]

3

Ambassador

"So we are Christ's ambassadors; God is making his appeal through us. We speak for Christ when we plead, "Come back to God!" For God made Christ, who never sinned, to be the offering for our sin, so that we could be made right with God through Christ."
[2 Corinthians 5:20-21 NLT]

AN AMBASSADOR IS:

1. Messenger.

2. Interpreter.

3. A representative of something/someone.

4. Entrusted - given authority by authority.

5. Responsible.

6. Wise - has integrity- knowing right, doing right.

7. Protective- defending its cause when needed.

8. Promoter-publicist.

9. Sent.

10. Influential.

AN AMBASSADOR SAYS:

1. **Whatever it takes.**
2. **Count me in.**
3. **Yes!**
4. **Your will God, not mine.**
5. **Your words God, not mine.**
6. **By the authority entrusted to me by God.**
7. **In the name of Jesus.**
8. **Here I am.**
9. **I am listening.**
10. **All for Your cause.**

"And He called to Him the Twelve [apostles] and began to send them out [as His ambassadors] two by two and gave them authority and power over the unclean spirits."
[Mark 6:7 AMP]

AN AMBASSADOR ACTS:

1. Delivers the message.
2. Goes out, highways and byways.
3. Does the hard yards; lasts the distance.
4. Foreruns.
5. Speaks up.
6. Steps out.
7. Stands out.
8. Leads the way.
9. Assumes his position.
10. His actions reflect his character.

> "Then he told servants, 'We have a wedding banquet all prepared but no guests. The ones I invited weren't up to it. Go out into the busiest intersections in town and invite anyone you find to the banquet.' The servants went out on the streets and rounded up everyone they laid eyes on, good and bad, regardless. And so the banquet was on- every place filled."
> Matthew 22:8-10 [Message]

4

An Excellent Attitude

1. Christ-like.
2. Encouraging.
3. Pioneering.
4. Renewed regularly.
5. Refreshes others.
6. Creates an environment of excellent living.
7. Gives courage and builds confidence.
8. Looks beyond the present circumstance.
9. Protects against offense.
10. Sees the best in people.
11. Takes personal responsibility.
12. Has an eternity perspective.
13. No matter what!
14. Holds no good thing back.
15. Seeks to understand.

Assets and Liabilities

10 MINISTRY ASSETS:

1. When we give
   Honoring God with ALL areas of your life.

2. When we pray
   Assuming a posture of prayer.

3. When we love the House of God
   Building the local church.

4. When we worship
   In Spirit and in truth.

5. When we read the Word of God
   Read, believe, obey.

6. When we disciple others
   Train up the next generation.

7. When we exercise discretion
   Everything is permissible, but not always profitable.

8. When we serve
   Jesus came to serve, not to be served.

9. When we have integrity
   Knowing right and doing right.

10. When we have energy
    Sow energy, reap energy.

10 MINISTRY LIABILITIES:

1. When we are selfish
   Insisting on personal rights.

2. When we people please
   Catering to public opinion.

3. When we know right and do wrong
   Character inconsistencies.

4. When we neglect our health
   Body + soul + spirit.

5. When we fear
   Being afraid of people.

6. When we are distracted
   Lack of focus.

7. When we are fragile
   Easily offended.

8. When we are lazy
   Allergic to hard work.

9. When we are critical
   Speaking negatively about people and ministry.

10. When we neglect our family
    Hiding behind ministry.

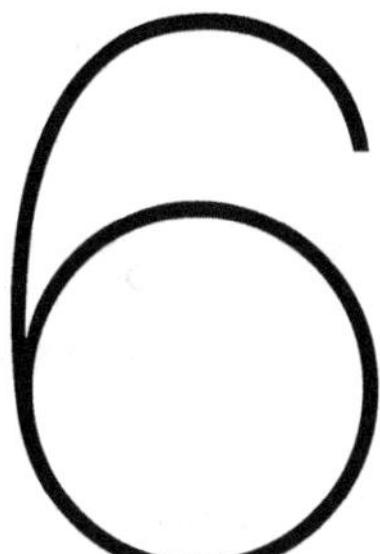

Bible Characters I Want to Meet

1. **Moses**
   I want to ask him how he handled not wanting to just kill everyone for being so disobedient and childlike.

2. **David**
   The warrior and worshiper; the shepherd and king.

3. **Peter**
   He was bold, outspoken, fearful yet fearless.

4. **Job**
   A man of great suffering who never cursed God.

5. **Solomon**
   Teach me everything you know please!

6. **Paul**
   To be a fly on the wall in the room where he prays.

7. **John**
   What did he do to be called 'The Beloved'?

8. **Joseph**
   Talk about an interesting life...he would win in any conversation about that!

9. **Jacob**
   Life before and after the wrestling match with God.

10. **Jesus**
    To meet THE MAN who laid down his life for me.

Bible Characters I Want to Meet

11. Mary
    I would ask her how she raised her children.

12. Esther
    Her first act of bravery was joining the harem!

13. Abigail
    Diplomat.

14. The woman caught in the act of adultery.
    I would love to know her name.

15. The widow who gave two copper coins.
    Her faith has helped to build my faith.

16. Jezebel
    If she could start again, would she change anything?

17. Eve
    Would love to know what a life without fear is like.

18. Rachel
    Her relationship with Leah after Jacob married her.

19. Sarah
    How she bounced back after childbirth!

20. Queen of Sheba
    Life before and after meeting King Solomon.

7

Bible Trivia

"...Always be prepared to give an answer to everyone who asks you to give the reason for the hope that you have. But do this with gentleness and respect..."
[1 Peter 3:15 NIV]

QUESTIONS:

1. What is the only domesticated animal not mentioned in the Bible?

2. What word appears exactly 1732 times in the New Living Translation Bible?

3. Which woman married Moses: Rahab, Jezebel, Michal or Zipporah?

4. What Arab State has the highest percentage of Christians?

5. What symbol did St. Patrick use to explain his theory of the Holy Trinity?

6. David's original wife was: Miriam, Michal, Leah or Bathsheba?

7. Jacob worked 7 years for the hand of: Rachel, Isabel, Gomer or Hagar?

8. What biblical place name means "pleasure"?

9. What animal is mentioned most frequently in both the New and Old Testaments?

10. What does an ecclesiophobic evangelist fear?

11. How much time did Jonah spend in the belly of the whale?

12. According to the Bible, what substance was used to seal the basket in which the infant Moses was set adrift on the Nile?

13. What language is Jesus believed to have spoken?

14. According to the Bible, what weapons was the Philistine giant Goliath carrying when he was slain by David?

15. According to the Bible, how many pearly gates are there?

16. Who were the parents of King Solomon?

17. How many books of the Bible are named after women?

18. In the Old Testament, who was Jezebel's husband?

19. Who was the disciple that was referred to as the one that Jesus loved?

20. Who was the youngest son of Jacob?

ANSWERS:

1. A Cat.
2. Give.
3. Zipporah.
4. Lebanon.
5. The Shamrock.
6. Michal.
7. Rachel.
8. Eden.
9. Sheep.
10. Churches.
11. Three days and three nights.
12. Pitch, or natural asphalt.
13. Aramaic
14. A sword and a spear.
15. 12.
16. David and Bathsheba.
17. Ruth and Esther.
18. Ahab, King of Israel.
19. John.
20. Benjamin.

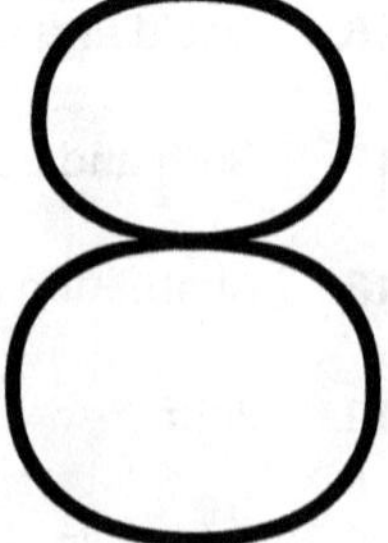

Body & Soul

After the birth of our youngest daughter, London Eternity, I had to face the daunting task of losing 75 pounds that I had gained during pregnancy [and nursing]. I reached my goal in just over 6 months and wrote a book, "Body & Soul" to help inspire others that they too can achieve their body and soul goals.

Most of us crave chocolate more than we crave freedom! We go for the quick fix. Instant gratification: short-term gain [the taste of chocolate] and long-term pain [a life of out-of-control eating]. Why? Because as human beings we do what we know we shouldn't do and we don't do what we know we should do. We know what is good and what is bad, but we need to get free. True freedom is about being comfortable in your own skin. We need to understand that we need help from a higher source!

> "Beloved one, I pray to God and wish on account of each and every bit of your life, regarding all things, that you, loved one, have a successful life and journey, and that your body be free from injury and disease, that you are sound and well, in direct proportion to having your mind, will and emotions prospered and flourishing."
>
> [3 John 1:3 personally paraphrased]

That is my prayer for you – that you would know that God is with you, Body & Soul, and that with every prayer you pray and every effort you put in, He will be there to partner with you to help you achieve your goals. I know because I couldn't have done what I have done without Him!

7 BASIC BODY & SOUL KEYS TO REMEMBER:

1. **If you eat often, you will help burn fat.**

2. **By increasing your lean protein intake, you will maintain muscle, and you will help burn fat.**

3. **By cutting down on starchy and sugary carbohydrates, you will store less fat.**

4. **Do steady, focused exercise, and you will burn fat and shape up.**

5. **Walk and pray – do both and you will prosper, Body & Soul.**

6. **If you can lose 5 pounds, you can lose 10, and if you can lose 10 pounds, you can lose 15, and if you can lose 20 pounds, you can lose anything!**

7. **The combination of walking and weights are a winning weight loss partnership. Do both and love the results.**

> "... I've tried everything and nothing helps. I'm at the end of my rope. Is there no one who can do anything for me? Isn't that the real question? The answer, thank God, is that Jesus Christ can and does. He acted to set things right in this life of contradictions..."
> [Romans 7 in The Message]

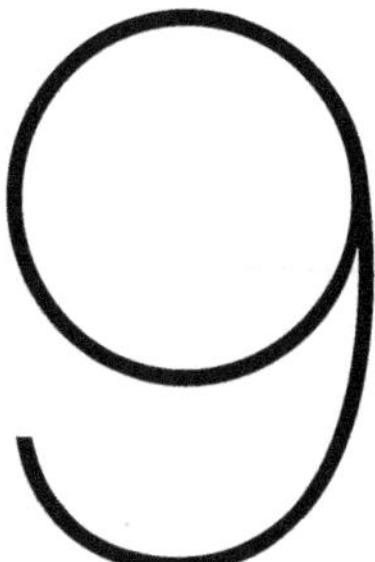

Called But Not Choosing

Do you ever wonder why some people don't want to be in full-time ministry, even if they are called?

1. Fear

   People may feel as though their own dreams won't come to pass if they 'set aside' their dreams for the Kingdom of God. In reality however, the Bible says in 1 Corinthians 2:9, "No eye has seen, no ear has heard, no mind has conceived what God has prepared for those who love Him."

2. Doubt

   People doubt their ability and capacity. They might have a fear that they aren't worthy, like Moses did. But they need to read the whole story.

3. Procrastination

   Answering the call of God takes obedience. And most people do not want to disobey God. So if they say yes, then that requires action. So they procrastinate, hoping God might change his mind.

4. Cost

   Ministry requires time, talent and treasure. Investing into people is a lot more time and energy consuming than any other project. However, people are eternal, money is not.

5. Independence

   Some people don't like authority; they prefer not to be kept accountable. The thought of being part of a star team isn't as attractive to them as being the star.

6. Grip

   The Bible says it is not until you lose your life for His sake that you will find it. People can't seem to wrap their head around that one. But faith says you don't need to. Just go!

7. Money

   The fear of not having enough money. Or the love of money.

8. Mess

   People are messy, and most people don't want to get their hands dirty.

9. Interruption

   Jesus rarely went anywhere without being interrupted. I think some people don't like change. And a life of ministry means things can change any minute, because people are constantly changing.

10. Blindness

    People who are called into full time ministry are just ordinary people, so it's hard for them to see how important they really are. However, they need to look at themselves with a vision for eternity rather than their own.

"Let us not become weary in doing good, for at the proper time we will reap a harvest if we do not give up."
[Galatians 6:9 NIV]

10

Characteristics of Character

10 CHARACTERISTICS OF A FOLLOWER:

1. Ability to listen.
2. Ability to submit.
3. Ability to trust.
4. Ability to get in line.
5. Supporting.
6. Available.
7. Right place, right time.
8. Understands the power of proximity.
9. Knows their place.
10. Willing and able to learn.

> "But Ruth said, 'Don't force me to leave you; don't make me go home. Where you go, I go; and where you live, I'll live. Your people are my people, you God is my god; where you die, I'll die, and that's where I'll be buried, so help me God- not even death itself is going to come between us!"
> [Ruth 1:15-18 The Message]

10 CHARACTERISTICS OF FAMILY:

1. **Understanding.**

2. **Sharing.**

3. **Conversation.**

4. **Security and trust.**

5. **Fun.**

6. **Food.**

7. **Mess.**

8. **Bond.**

9. **Ages and stages of life.**

10. **Forgiving.**

> **"In some families, 'please' is described as the magic word. In our house however, it was 'sorry'."**
>
> **- Margaret Laurance**

10 CHARACTERISTICS OF A FRIEND:

1. Defends when needed.

2. Believes in you.

3. Can lower you through the roof on your mat at any time.

4. Encourages.

5. Challenges.

6. Speaks the truth in love.

7. Gives.

8. Takes.

9. Responds.

10. Available.

"How well God must like you— you don't hang out at Sin Saloon, you don't slink along Dead-End Road, you don't go to Smart-Mouth College. Instead you thrill to God's Word, you chew on Scripture day and night."
[Psalm 1:1-2 The Message]

10 CHARACTERISTICS OF A FAN:

1. Supportive.

2. Causes positive activity.

3. Believer.

4. Spreads the word.

5. Enthusiastic.

6. Refresher.

7. Gatherer.

8. Carries the message wherever they go.

9. Promotes.

10. Knows all the details: date, time, place!

> "Then, leaving her water jar, the woman went back to the town and said to the people, 'Come, see a man who told me everything I ever did. Could this be the Christ?' They came out of town and made their way toward him."
> [John 4:28-30 NIV]

10 CHARACTERISTICS OF A FOE:

"You have enemies? Good. That means you've stood up for something, sometime in your life."
- Winston Churchill

1. Adverse.
2. Antagonizing.
3. Intimidating.
4. Irritating.
5. Opposing.
6. Negative.
7. Weak.
8. Arrogant.
9. Dangerous.
10. Accuser.

"A man who was completely innocent, offered himself as a sacrifice for the good of others, including his enemies, and became the ransom of the world. It was a perfect act."
- Mohandas Gandhi

11

Circles of Love

> "There's trouble ahead when you live only for the approval of others, saying what flatters them, doing what indulges them. Popularity contests are not truth contests—look how many scoundrel preachers were approved by your ancestors! Your task is to be true, not popular."
> [Luke 6:26 The Message]

The relationships in our life fall into circles of connection that we create. As leaders it is vital to have appropriate boundaries to help us help ourselves and others. If you are married, then you and your husband's intimate relationship as a married couple is the closest circle you have, then your children, then your closest friends, family, associates, etc.

Jesus made it clear that we should love our enemies, which means they somehow need to fall within a circle of love in our life. This however doesn't mean they belong close, it just means they still belong somewhere in your sphere of love.

Your own personal circles of connections are vital to your leadership and where and how you can be utilized. If your relationships are primarily with negative people [even if you are trying to help them], then sooner or later their negative influence will affect and contaminate your life and relationships. This is the "guilty by association leadership principle" that every leader needs to be aware of.

Remember what the Bible says in Luke 6:26 in The Message, "Popularity contests are not truth contests."

Show me your friends, and I will show you your future!

As leaders IT'S TIME to realize:

1. **My path determines my proximity as a leader to leaders above me and leaders beside me.**

2. **My proximity as a leader, to people in my world, determines my purpose as a leader.**

3. **My purpose determines my prosperity as a leader: body + soul + spirit**

> **"LORD, you alone are my portion and my cup; you make my lot secure. The boundary lines have fallen for me in pleasant places; surely I have a delightful inheritance. I will praise the LORD, who counsels me; even at night my heart instructs me."**
>
> **[Psalm 16:5-7 NIV]**

12

Committed Communicator

A commitment to communicate says you value the relationship. We need to be committed to healthy communication every single day. Even if we're having a bad day, we need a good strategy. If we can't communicate effectively, respectfully, clearly, then we will always be frustrated with others and ourselves. When we place a higher expectation on others understanding us than we place on understanding others, there will be a gulf of disappointment created in our lives.

I believe it is our responsibility to work on our communication skills so much so that it is something we should never stop working on – our whole lives.

To communicate means...

1. To express thoughts.

2. To express feelings.

3. To express information.

4. To express easily or effectively.

5. To express oneself in such a way that one is readily and clearly understood.

6. To be connected, one with another.

7. Communion.

13

Common Ground

> "Even though I am a free man with no master, I have become a slave to all people to bring many to Christ. When I was with the Jews, I lived like a Jew to bring the Jews to Christ. When I was with those who follow the Jewish law, I too lived under that law. Even though I am not subject to the law, I did this so I could bring to Christ those who are under the law. When I am with the Gentiles who do not follow the Jewish law, I too live apart from that law so I can bring them to Christ. But I do not ignore the law of God; I obey the law of Christ. When I am with those who are weak, I share their weakness, for I want to bring the weak to Christ. Yes, I try to find common ground with everyone, doing everything I can to save some. I do everything to spread the Good News and share in its blessings."
> [1 Corinthians 9:19-23 NLT]

As leaders our relationships are more than 'friendships'. I have two very close friends that I have had for over 25 years. One of my friends shares my belief in Jesus Christ and the other is still on the journey of discovery. What I love most about being friends with these women is the diversity they bring to my life. We have shared values (common ground) that help us focus on what is important.

As leaders, I pray we learn to start leading with our lives when it comes to building healthy relationships.

Can we please start to lead with our lives?

IT'S TIME!

7 COMMON GROUNDS:

1. Common Purpose vs Common Pleasure
   - purpose builds our lives and God's kingdom
   - pleasure lasts for a moment

2. Common Pressure vs Common Problem
   - pressure builds our character and capacity
   - problems are for solving not for consoling

3. Common Passion vs Common Pursuits
   - passion for God's House should consume us
   - pursuits for anything else will only distract us

4. Common Promotion vs Common Prima Donnas
   - promotion requires discretion
   - prima donnas expect to be noticed

5. Common Privilege vs Common Poverty
   - privilege shares
   - poverty stores

6. Common Progress vs Common Pitfalls
   - progress is evident to all
   - pitfalls hold us back

7. Common Practice vs Common Publicity
   - practices what is preached
   - publicity says, "Do as I say but don't do as I do."

14

Cross Examine My Heart

[or rub me up the wrong way and see if I purr]

The psalmist David asked the Lord to do a very interesting thing in Psalm 26 and again in Psalm 139, when he asked to be 'cross-examined' by God. How often are we prepared to be 'cross-examined' by God to see what's really going on in our heart? One of the greatest fears of any person is the fear of being misunderstood or misrepresented. When we live with this fear it causes us to be defensive and the last thing we would want to happen is to be 'cross-examined' by God or anyone else. Perhaps IT'S TIME to allow your velvet heart to be rubbed in both directions to see what's really inside!

> "Declare me innocent, O Lord, for I have acted with integrity; I have trusted in the Lord without wavering. Put me on trial, Lord, and cross-examine me. Test my motives and my heart. For I am always aware of your unfailing love, and I have lived according to your truth."
> [Psalm 26:1-3 NLT]

> "Investigate my life, O God, find out everything about me; cross-examine and test me, get a clear picture of what I'm about; see for yourself whether I've done anything wrong then guide me on the road to eternal life."
> [Psalm 139:23-24 The Message]

> "Many a man proclaims his own loving-kindness and goodness, but a faithful man who can find?"
> [Proverbs 20:6 Amplified Bible]

Has anyone or anything wound you up the wrong way lately?

1. Friends
   [your friends playing hokey pokey with you]

2. Finance
   [the cost of being a leader in the Kingdom]

3. Family
   [family can provide a smooth option when Kingdom life seems rough]

4. Failure
   [pride goes before a fall, so humble yourself in time and failure doesn't mean you'll fall over]

5. Fatigue
   [lack of sleep gives you lack of perspective]

> "As iron sharpens iron, so a friend sharpens a friend."
> [Proverbs 27:17 NLT]

The truth is, if we don't allow life to sharpen us, then we will end up taking the bait called "offense". So how do we "offense-proof" our life? We have to know who we are so that we can respond in the right way even when we are being rubbed up the wrong way.

We need to learn from the Master's example. Jesus didn't react to their accusations. Jesus responded with who He is and not what He did. When we can be secure in who we are, we won't have to fight over 'he said', 'she said', 'they said'. Remember, he, she and they will always have something to say!

> "Inside, the leading priests and the entire high council were trying to find witnesses who would lie about Jesus, so they could put him to death. But even though they found many who agreed to give false witness, they could not use anyone's testimony. Finally, two men came forward who declared, "This man said, 'I am able to destroy the Temple of God and rebuild it in three days.'" Then the high priest stood up and said to Jesus, "Well, aren't you going to answer these charges? What do you have to say for yourself?" But Jesus remained silent. Then the high priest said to him, "I demand in the name of the living God—tell us if you are the Messiah, the Son of God." Jesus replied, "You have said it. And in the future you will see the Son of Man seated in the place of power at God's right hand and coming on the clouds of heaven."
> [Matthew 26:59-70 NLT]

Our relationships aren't solid until they have been tested. Maybe you are going through some of those tests right now. See it as being an opportunity to allow your heart to be 'cross-examined'. Use this season as an opportunity to learn and grow. After a while, the same things that hurt, annoy, frustrate, distract and bother you now, won't have the same affect in the future, if you choose to be changed and sharpened in the process of 'cross-examination'.

Let's jump on board the grace train because it's always moving forward, there's always room for you and me and there's always room for change. Let's lower our expectations and let's raise our tolerance. Let's be committed to getting to know each other better. To know is to love.

IT'S TIME to get the love back!

15

Debt Reduction

> "Don't run up debts, except for the huge debt of love you owe each other. When you love others, you complete what the law has been after all along. The law code—don't sleep with another person's spouse, don't take someone's life, don't take what isn't yours, don't always be wanting what you don't have, and any other "don't" you can think of—finally adds up to this: Love other people as well as you do yourself. You can't go wrong when you love others. When you add up everything in the law code, the sum total is love."
> [Romans 13:8-10 The Message]

7 KEYS TO DEBT REDUCTION:

1. Tithe.

2. Give.

3. Steward.

4. Save.

5. Find a better paying job.

6. Work out a plan.

7. Live within your budget.

16

Deference vs Defensiveness

"Some time later two prostitutes came to the king to have an argument settled. "Please, my lord," one of them began, "this woman and I live in the same house. I gave birth to a baby while she was with me in the house. Three days later this woman also had a baby. We were alone; there were only two of us in the house. "But her baby died during the night when she rolled over on it. Then she got up in the night and took my son from beside me while I was asleep. She laid her dead child in my arms and took mine to sleep beside her. And in the morning when I tried to nurse my son, he was dead! But when I looked more closely in the morning light, I saw that it wasn't my son at all." Then the other woman interrupted, "It certainly was your son, and the living child is mine." "No," the first woman said, "the living child is mine, and the dead one is yours." And so they argued back and forth before the king. Then the king said, "Let's get the facts straight. Both of you claim the living child is yours, and each says that the dead one belongs to the other. All right, bring me a sword." So a sword was brought to the king. Then he said, "Cut the living child in two, and give half to one woman and half to the other!" Then the woman who was the real mother of the living child, and who loved him very much, cried out, "Oh no, my lord! Give her the child—please do not kill him!" But the other woman said, "All right, he will be neither yours nor mine; divide him between us!" Then the king said, "Do not kill the child, but give him to the woman who wants him to live, for she is his mother!" When all Israel heard the king's decision, the people were in awe of the king, for they saw the wisdom God had given him for rendering justice."
[1 Kings 3:16-28 Amplified Bible]

10 DIFFERENCES BETWEEN THE TWO MOTHERS:

1. **Responsibility vs Abdication.**
2. **Reacting in haste vs Responding in love.**
3. **Selflessness vs Selfishness.**
4. **Righteous anger vs Jealousy.**
5. **Caution vs Negligence.**
6. **Compassion vs Callousness.**
7. **Conditional vs Unconditional.**
8. **Devotion vs Fickleness.**
9. **Patience vs Intolerance.**
10. **Acceptance vs Regret.**

Destiny Relationships

1. Adam & Eve
   Humanity was birthed.

2. Paul & Peter
   15 days of destiny exchange [Galatians 1:18].

3. Naomi & Ruth
   Loyalty led to the coming of Christ.

4. Joseph & Pharoah
   Powerful leadership is exemplified.

5. Elizabeth & Mary
   They birthed the forerunner AND the Savior!

6. Esther & Mordecai
   He spoke up, then she spoke up, and both won favor.

7. Moses & Jethro
   Together they developed a radical new way of leading.

8. Nehemiah & The King
   They exemplified the privilege and the responsibility of personal service.

9. Elijah & Elisha
   The were the original apprenticeship relationship.

10. Paul & Timothy
    Every great teacher needs a great student.

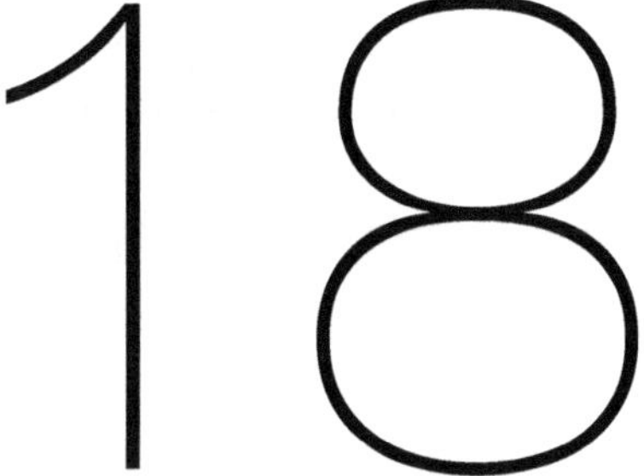

Destructive Relationships

1. Ahab and Jezebel [1 Kings 21:5-16]
   Death of Naboth (an innocent man).

2. Judas and the Pharisees [Matthew 14-16, 27:3-5]
   Betrayal and death of Christ.

3. Lot and his Daughters [Genesis 19:30-38]
   Moabites and Ammonites brought grief and war to the Israelites for generations.

4. Job and his Friends [Book of Job]
   Fair-weather friends.

5. David and Bathsheba [2 Samuel 1]
   Brought death of an innocent man.

6. Ananias and Sapphira [Acts 5:1-11]
   Lying about money brought their instant death.

7. Sampson and Delilah [Judges 16:4-21]
   Had his eyes gouged out.

8. Herodias and Herod Antipas [Mark 6:21-29]
   Death of John the Baptist.

9. Rehoboam and Friends [1 Kings 12:1-19]
   Spilt of Judah and Israel.

10. Eve and the Serpent [Genesis 3:1-19]
    The fall of mankind.

19

Devotion

"All the believers devoted themselves to the apostles' teaching, and to fellowship, and to sharing in meals (including the Lord's Supper), and to prayer. A deep sense of awe came over them all, and the apostles performed many miraculous signs and wonders. And all the believers met together in one place and shared everything they had. They sold their property and possessions and shared the money with those in need. They worshiped together at the Temple each day, met in homes for the Lord's Supper, and shared their meals with great joy and generosity all the while praising God and enjoying the goodwill of all the people. And each day the Lord added to their fellowship those who were being saved."
[Acts 2:42-47 NLT]

DEVOTION DEFINED:

- Zealous
- Attached
- Loyal
- Affectionate
- Friend
- Constant
- Devout
- Concerned
- Fond
- Faithful
- Loving
- True
- Attentive
- Supportive
- Dedicated

- Committed
- Keen
- Enthusiastic
- Single-minded
- Focused
- Interested
- Invested

When we understand the meaning of devotion, it's important for us to know what the opposite of devotion is:

- Uncaring
- Uncommitted
- Unenthusiastic

When we are devoted we accept and welcome leadership opportunities, challenge and change. We become 'yes and amen' leaders. When we are devoted we say 'count me in' with a 'bring it on' spirit. Without a 'bring it on' spirit, our devotion is unsustainable.

Devotion is drawn by the Holy Spirit in our lives; devotion isn't about our personal ability to be disciplined. It is the posture and purpose of our heart.

> "And I tell you, you are Peter [Greek, Petros--a large piece of rock], and on this rock [Greek, petra--a huge rock like Gibraltar] I will build My church, and the gates of Hades (the powers of the infernal region) shall not overpower it [or be strong to its detriment or hold out against it]."
> [Matthew 16:18 AMP]

Jesus said He will build His church and upon our revelation we will be part of it. Let's be aware of the enemy's plan to distract us from our devotion to God and His purpose for our lives.

IT'S TIME to wise up!

20

Double Trouble

> "Here are six things God hates, and one more that he loathes with a passion; eyes that are arrogant, a tongue that lies, hands that murder the innocent, a heart that hatches evil plots, feet that race down a wicked track, a mouth that lies under oath, a troublemaker in the family."
> [Proverbs 6:16-19 The Message]

WHAT GOD HATES:

1. Eyes that are arrogant.
2. A tongue that lies.
3. Hands that murder the innocent.
4. A heart that hatches evil plots.
5. Feet that race down a wicked track.
6. A mouth that lies under oath.

WHAT GOD LOATHES WITH A PASSION:

7. A troublemaker in the family.

We know how painful it is when someone causes trouble in our lives. It isn't surprising therefore when the Bible says that God "loathes with a passion" a troublemaker in the family. The thing that causes us the most trouble is usually our mouths and the words that we speak. Can you recall a time when the words of your mouth caused trouble in your family? I'm sure you can think of many times when the words of others have caused trouble in your family at home or in your church family. A trouble maker in the family upsets people on earth, and they upset God in heaven. That's what I call 'Double Trouble'! For us to ensure that we aren't causing 'Double Trouble' we need to be wise with our words. We need to take care not to have big mouths!

Following are 15 things that God loves:

1. **The Holy Spirit's presence in our life**
   [it is there or it is not - He dwells or He does not]

   "But the Holy Spirit produces this kind of fruit in our lives: love, joy, peace, patience, kindness, goodness, faithfulness, gentleness, and self-control. There is no law against these things!
   [Galatians 5:22-23 NLT]

2. **Family**
   [common/community]

   "(Words Kill, Words Give Life) Loners who care only for themselves spit on the common good."
   [Proverbs 18:1 The Message]

3. **Humility**
   [Godly confidence]

   "Lift not up your [aggressive] horn on high, speak not with a stiff neck and insolent arrogance. For not from the east nor from the west nor from the south come promotion and lifting up. But God is the Judge! He puts down one and lifts up another."
   [Psalm 75:5-7 AMP]

3. **Discernment**
   [knowing what, when, who]

   "Wisdom is found on the lips of the discerning, but a rod is for the back of one who has no sense. The wise store up knowledge, but the mouth of a fool invites ruin."
   [Proverbs 10:13-14 NIV]

4. Protection
[guard/protect/watch over/be vigilant/don't let out]

"He who guards his mouth keeps his life, but he who opens wide his lips comes to ruin."
[Proverbs 13:3 AMP]

5. Selection
[selective hearing/selective listening/stay far away]

"The words of a fool start fights; do him a favor and gag him. Fools are undone by their big mouths; their souls are crushed by their words. Listening to gossip is like eating cheap candy; do you really want junk like that in your belly?"
[Proverbs 18:6-8 The Message]

6. Reputation
[as determined by others]

"Let someone else praise you, and not your own mouth; an outsider, and not your own lips."
[Proverbs 27:2 NIV]

7. Measure
[more quality/less quantity]

"The more talk, the less truth; the wise measure their words."
[Proverbs 10:19 The Message]

8. Care
[laundry care cycle/separate delicate from durable]

"The good acquire a taste for helpful conversation; bullies push and shove their way through life. Careful words make for a careful life; careless talk may ruin everything."
[Proverbs 13:2-3 The Message]

9. Kindness
[causing attachment or causing detachment]

"God doesn't miss a thing— he's alert to good and evil alike. Kind words heal and help; cutting words wound and maim."
[Proverbs 15:3-4 The Message]

9. Cultivation
[growth in integrity]

"Good leaders cultivate honest speech; they love advisors who tell them the truth."
[Proverbs 16:13 The Message]

10. Intelligence
[mind in gear before mouth in drive]

"True intelligence is a spring of fresh water, while fools sweat it out the hard way. They make a lot of sense, these wise folks; whenever they speak, their reputation increases. Gracious speech is like clover honey— good taste to the soul, quick energy for the body."
[Proverbs 16:22-24 The Message]

11. Resistance
[stop the spread]

"Mean people spread mean gossip; their words smart and burn.'
[Proverbs 16:27 The Message]

12. Truth
[integrity]

"In a lawsuit the first to speak seems right, until someone comes forward and cross-examines."
[Proverbs 18: 18 NIV]

13. Fruit
[words that bring life not death]

"Words kill, words give life; they're either poison or fruit—you choose."
[Proverbs 18:21 The Message]

14. Restraint
[bit and bridle style!]

"Watch your words and hold your tongue; you'll save yourself a lot of grief."
[Proverbs 21:23 The Message]

15. Longevity
[be more than a 'one time' wonder]

"Truthful lips endure forever, but a lying tongue lasts only a moment."
[Proverbs 12:19 NIV]

21

Dream Destinations

Just as there are many dream destinations or vacation spots, there are other dream destinations we should focus on as leaders. When it comes to dreaming about Hawaii, Cancun, Europe, Australia, or anywhere else that might be a favorite destination, we tend to spend quality time and energy planning to achieve the ultimate vacation goal. We need to focus our time and energy on more than vacations that last a moment. We can reach dream destinations with our lives that last for time and eternity.

Where do you want your life to be in the future? Next month? A year from now? 5 years from now? 10 years from now? 25 years from now? If we play the movie of our life out (hypothetically speaking), we arrive at a set of outcomes.

We will arrive at those outcomes as a direct result of our objectives (what we aim for) and our strategy (what we plan for). We can aim for anything but we should plan for everything. We can't simply aim and arrive. We need to practice the "Ready, Set, Go" leadership principle.

Have we counted the cost of life and leadership?

IT'S TIME!

> "Suppose one of you want to build a tower. Will he not first sit down and estimate the cost to see if he has enough money to complete it? For if he lays the foundation and is not able to finish it, everyone who sees it will ridicule him, saying, 'This fellow began to build and was not able to finish."
>
> [Luke 14:28-30 NIV]

Effective Communication

1. Wise Up!

   Read your Bible and pray every day. Reading the book of Proverbs over and over and over again will change your life! As leaders, we can all afford to wise up!

   "Solomon speaking..."Now, O Lord God, let Your promise to David my father be fulfilled, for you have made me king over a people like the dust of the earth in multitude. Give me now wisdom and knowledge to go out and come in before this people, for who can rule this Your people who are so great? God replied to Solomon, Because this was in your heart and you have not asked for riches, possessions, honor, and glory, or the life of your foes, or even for long life, but have asked wisdom and knowledge for yourself, that you may rule and judge My people over whom I have made you king, Wisdom and knowledge are granted you. And I will give you riches, possessions, honor, and glory, such as none of the kings had before you, and none after you shall have their equal."
   [2 Chronicles 1:9-12 AMP]

2. Choose the right moment and the right place.

   If you need to discuss something in private with a person, make sure that the choice of venue is private and that you do not feel uncomfortable about the possibility of being overheard. Or, if you need to make your point before a group of people, ensure that the location is somewhere that your discussion will be able to be heard by all who are present and make sure you captivate each and every person in the group.

3. **Think yourself clear before you attempt to communicate.**
   If you are feeling passionate about what you are trying to communicate, you may sound confused if you haven't already thought of some key points to stick with. Know your 'theme' and maybe choose three main points and keep your communication focused on those.

4. Stay on-subject.
   Make sure all facts and stories actually add to your conversation. And don't be afraid to reuse key phrases throughout your conversation, so long as they are constructive and not argumentative.

5. Be clear about the purpose of the communication.
   For example, your purpose could be to inform others, to obtain information or to initiate action. You need to have worked this out in advance.

6. Engage Effectively
   Be articulate and try not to mumble. Look into the other person's eyes. Use facial expressions consciously, and please remember to come up for breath!

7. Be aware of Body Language
   Be conscious of what your hands are saying as you speak. Some hand gestures are ineffective or intimidating, and please try to be still and not fidgety.

8. Remove distractions.
   Turn off your cell phone. Choose somewhere to talk that doesn't have loud music or noisy people! And stay focused even if there are distractions around you.

9. Listen.
   Be attentive when listening and ensure that your facial expressions reflect your interest. Communication is a two-way street and requires us to listen as well. Remember, while we are talking we are not learning. It can be helpful to ask the person you are talking to rephrase some of what you have said in their own words to see how clear or confused they are.

10. Thank the person for their time to listen and respond.
    No matter what the outcome of your communication, even if the response to your conversation has been negative, it is important to end it on a good note. Saying "Thank you", regardless, goes a long way to convey respect and love.

> "Speak up for those who cannot speak for themselves; ensure justice for those being crushed. Yes, speak up for the poor and helpless, and see that they get justice."
> [Proverbs 31:8-9 NLT]

We won't have any hope of anyone listening to us 'speaking up' if they cannot understand what we are saying. Let's be committed to healthy communication.

IT'S TIME!

23

Enemies of Devotion

1. DEVIL [seek to kill & destroy]
   who tells you anything twisted.

2. Distrust
   that tells you can only trust God and not people.

3. Discouragement
   that tells you to sit down inside and shut up.

4. Distraction
   that tells you to keep your options open.

5. Disappointment
   that tells you to protect yourself.

6. Distance
   that tells you to play it safe.

7. Doubt
   that tells you to question everyone and everything.

8. Double-Mindedness
   that tells you to live in confusion.

9. Disbelief
   that tells you facts are greater than TRUTH.

10. Division
    that tells you to draw your own following.

11. **Disillusion**
    that tells you how blind else everyone is but you.

12. **Delusion**
    that tells you don't need anyone but God.

13. **Dating**
    that tells you to play the field.

14. **Debt**
    that tells you to stop you giving to God.

15. **Dread**
    that tells you to stay away not draw near.

"The discipline of daily devotion to God undergirds all decisions."
- Edwin Louis Cole

24

Exemplary Leadership Values

1. **Self-motivation**
   No one has to stir me up.

2. **Self-informed**
   No one has to remind me.

3. **Self-initiated**
   Taking responsibility.

4. **Self-controlled**
   Fruit of the Spirit is evident.

5. **Self-regulated**
   Balancing the big life.

6. **Self-esteemed**
   Knowing my value in Christ.

7. **God-seeker**
   Relationship is rewarding.

8. **Risk-taker**
   Full of faith and wisdom.

9. **Ever-increasing capacity**
   Willingness to grow and learn.

10. **Cheerful Giver**
    Picking up the tab is a favorite past-time.

25

Fear Not

Don't worry about anything but pray about everything!

> "Do not fret or have any anxiety about anything, but in every circumstance and in everything, by prayer and petition (definite requests), with thanksgiving, continue to make your wants known to God. And God's peace [shall be yours, that tranquil state of a soul assured of its salvation through Christ, and so fearing nothing from God and being content with its earthly lot of whatever sort that is, that peace] which transcends all understanding shall garrison and mount guard over your hearts and minds in Christ Jesus."
> [Philippians 4:6-7 AMP]

10 CHARACTERISTICS OF FEAR:

1. Lack of love.
2. Crippling.
3. Distracting.
4. Misunderstanding.
5. Controlling.
6. No room for mistakes.
7. Anxiety.
8. Threatening.
9. Binding.
10. Vision blurring.

10 REASONS WHY WE FEAR:

1. Unknown territory.
2. Misunderstanding of expectation.
3. A scary experience.
4. Lack of preparation.
5. Failure.
6. Someone else's mistakes.
7. Not meeting standards.
8. Self- conscious.
9. When we don't read our Bible consistently.
10. Wrong belief system.

> "The fear of death follows from the fear of life. A man who lives fully is prepared to die at any time."
> - Mark Twain

10 REASONS WHY NOT TO FEAR:

1. Perfect love casts out all fear.
2. It doesn't add a minute to your life.
3. It doesn't stop the "problem"
4. It's the opposite of faith.
5. Grace prevails.
6. Remember, Jesus calms the storms.
7. The worst things in life can be overcome by faith.
8. It causes wrinkles. No one wants that.
9. It stops the flow of God in your life.
10. Robs you of peace and clear thinking space.

> "There is no fear in love [dread does not exist], but full-grown (complete, perfect) love turns fear out of doors and expels every trace of terror! For fear brings with it the thought of punishment, and [so] he who is afraid has not reached the full maturity of love [is not yet grown into love's complete perfection]."
>
> [1 John 4:18 Amplified Bible]

26

Focus

10 THINGS JESUS FOCUSED ON:

1. The will of His Father.
2. Humanity.
3. His mission.
4. Fulfilling prophecy.
5. Meeting need.
6. Bringing the Good News.
7. Discipleship.
8. His core three team.
9. Prayer - communication with the Father.
10. His Church.

"Aim at heaven and you will get the earth thrown in. Aim at earth and you will get neither."
- C.S. Lewis

10 THINGS PEOPLE FOCUS ON:

1. Money [what they don't have and what they do have].
2. Position.
3. Gift.
4. Recognition.
5. Receiving.
6. Short term outcomes.
7. Outward appearance.
8. Material things.
9. Tomorrow.
10. Unfinished business - dishes in the sink or laundry to be done.

> "If you decide for God, living a life of God-worship, it follows that you don't fuss about what's on the table at mealtimes or whether the clothes in your closet are in fashion. There is far more to your life than the food you put in your stomach, more to your outer appearance than the clothes you hang on your body. Look at the birds, free and unfettered, not tied down to a job description, careless in the care of God. And you count far more to him than birds."
> [Matthew 6:25-26 The Message]

27

Follow The Leader

> "SEEING THE crowds, He went up on the mountain; and when He was seated, His disciples came to Him. Then He opened His mouth and taught them..."
> [Matthew 5:1 AMP]

There are times in our life as leaders and followers that we take time out to teach and to be taught. When we are busily involved in the industry of ministry it is all too easy to presume that people who are following us understand why we do what we do.

The Industrial Revolution that arose from the 18th to the 19th Century helped with efficiency of time, talent and treasure. The work moved from labor intensive to mass production. That's awesome when it comes to making 'stuff' but not when it comes to people. As leaders we can't mass-produce leaders. Building people is labor intensive because that's the nature of LOVE.

We are called to see God's kingdom advance and grow. We are called to see our Church flourish and grow. We are called to see the individual call of God on our lives be fulfilled.

Even Jesus took His disciples aside and made time to explain things to them. They had been with Jesus and large crowds of people, watching Jesus interacting with people, healing the sick, performing miracles, and the disciples – Jesus' team were caught up in the midst of it all, much like we can be caught up in the midst of ministry. Sometimes we just need to sit and recapture why it is that we do what we do, so that every season in our lives can make sense and produce fruit.

Jesus wants us to follow Him – to be His disciples. He wants us to follow Him in word and in deed; that we would follow His example, listen to His words, do His work; that we would accept the will of His Father, and to fulfill His purpose for our lives. That we would become like Jesus.

As leaders we need to understand that delegation without responsibility is abdication. True discipleship is all about following Jesus and leading others to follow Him.

IT'S TIME to follow Him closer!

> **"Jesus refused. 'First things first. Your business is life, not death. Follow me. Pursue life.'"**
>
> **[Matthew 8:22 The Message]**

28

For Women Only

10 THINGS ONLY WOMEN UNDERSTAND
[emailed to me by a girlfriend...]

10. Why it's good to have five pairs of black shoes.

9. The difference between cream, ivory, and off-white.

8. Crying can be fun.

7. Fat clothes.

6. A salad, diet drink, and a hot fudge sundae make a balanced lunch.

5. Discovering a designer dress on the clearance rack can be considered a peak life experience.

4. The inaccuracy of every bathroom scale ever made.

3. A good man might be hard to find, but a good hairdresser is next to impossible.

2. Why a phone call between two women never lasts under ten minutes.

AND THE NUMBER ONE THING ONLY WOMEN UNDERSTAND:

1. OTHER WOMEN!

29

Gone AWOL

> "We should be too big to take offense and too noble to give it." - Abraham Lincoln

How do you know if you have gone AWOL?
[absent without leave]

1. You are offended.

2. You have a spirit of self-entitlement.

3. You act independently.

4. You focus on what's best for you, rather than what's best for everyone.

5. You find the need to justify everything you do.

6. You're restless.

7. You've traded in former convictions.

8. You've lost vision for your life.

9. Your loyalty has shifted.

10. People who were your friends, you now view as enemies.

> "If your boss [or leader] is angry at you, don't quit! A quiet spirit can overcome even great mistakes.
> [Ecclesiastes 10:4 NLT]

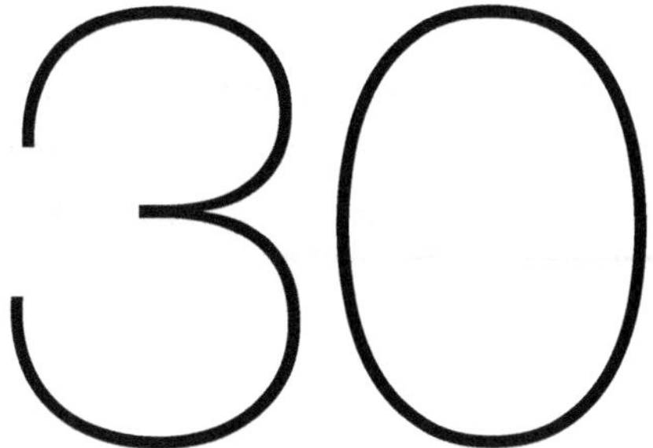

Good Cop, Bad Cop

Leadership is like a bus. Every leader jumps on board every day and there are always two seats to choose from:

1. GOOD COP
   Some leaders always like to sit in the good cop seat because they love to be loved. The Good Cop seat is the 'mercy' or 'clemency' seat where leadership is exercised to pardon.

2. BAD COP
   Other leaders like to sit in the bad cop seat because they love to confront. The Bad Cop seat is the 'justice' or 'truth' seat where leadership is exercised to correct.

I don't know many great leaders who love confrontation. However, great leaders are prepared to confront when necessary. Knowing the right time, the right place is essential. Working together as a leadership team is essential. We need to understand that the goal in dealing with difficult situations is to do our best as leaders not to lose people along the way. Relationship is more important than being 'right'.

Just remember, if you are the kind of leader who tends to always sit in the Good Cop seat, you are always providing the Bad Cop seat to another leader on your team. Have a conversation with your team-mates before you embark on the bus and work out the best strategy that will bring great fruit.

IT'S TIME!

31

Good to Great

God is good! When we learn to really live in His goodness, we can experience His greatness. Following are 7 keys to take us from GOOD to GREAT:

> "No doubt about it! God is good— good to good people, good to the good-hearted. But I nearly missed it, missed seeing his goodness. I was looking the other way, looking up to the people at the top, envying the wicked who have it made, who have nothing to worry about, not a care in the whole wide world."
> [Psalm 73:1-3 The Message]

1. PRIORITIES

   We need to get the order of our priorities right. Just like the Price is Right television game, we can have all the right things on the board, but have them all in the wrong order, and we won't get the grand prize in the end. Kingdom first means we don't need to worry when life, naturally speaking, 'zero's' out. There is power in 'zeroing' out so that real faith can kick in.

2. COMMUNICATION

   We need to do away with "He said", "She said", "They said". Next level leadership requires clear and effective communication, follow through and a high-completion drive. We need to strategize and process to achieve our objectives. Just like someone who wants to bake a cake needs a list of ingredients, they also need a method of construction before they can bake and enjoy how the cake tastes.

3. VISION

We all have a blind spot. Do you know what yours is? When we are driving we see through our windshield, back window, rear view mirror, windows, and side mirrors. We even turn our head to ensure we aren't going to hit someone when we change lanes. With all of these safety measures, we still need to acknowledge that blind spots exist when we are on the road, or we are likely to have a nasty accident. It's always good to ask someone who knows you to help you discover your blind spots so you can work on improving your visibility and accountability.

4. CAPACITY

How full is your tank? You can run on empty but you will eventually run out of gas. As leaders we need to take personal responsibility to look after ourselves – body+soul+spirit so that we can increase our capacity rather than just maintaining our capacity.

5. CHANGE

The Call of God doesn't drop in our inbox; it grows over time. We need to be prepared to be challenged, corrected and redirected, to face discomfort and choose to grow and learn in every season. The definition of "functional" is literally the ability to adapt. Dysfunctional leaders become stuck in a moment when they decide they aren't going to learn, grow and change anymore. The truth is, leaders who aren't prepared to change will eventually face change they cannot choose for themselves.

6. **INTEGRITY**

   My definition of integrity is simple: know right and do right. When we know right and do wrong, we compromise our integrity. As leaders we should be living lives of integrity both in our internal attitude and in our external behavior.

   "The path of life leads upward for the wise; they leave the grave behind."
   [Proverbs 15:24 NLT]

7. **RELATIONSHIPS**

   Who we spend our time with will influence our lives. The Bible is full of wisdom on relationships – the good, the bad and the ugly. We have all experienced good, bad and ugly relationships, and exercising wisdom is the only way to change and redirect our focus. We love all people, but we should only allow the uncompromised to influence our lives as leaders.

"Be not afraid of greatness; some are born great, some achieve greatness, and others have greatness thrust upon them."
William Shakespeare

32

Great Expectations

1. EXPECTATION OF A PERSON

"In the morning, O LORD, you hear my voice; in the morning I lay my requests before you and wait in expectation."
[Psalm 5:3 NLT]

2. EXPECTATION OF GOD

"My soul, wait only upon God and silently submit to Him; for my hope and expectation are from Him. He only is my Rock and my Salvation; He is my Defense and my Fortress, I shall not be moved."
[Psalm 62:5-6 AMP]

3. EXPECTATION OF A LEADER

"Even though I am free of the demands and expectations of everyone, I have voluntarily become a servant to any and all in order to reach a wide range of people: religious, nonreligious, meticulous moralists, loose-living immoralists, the defeated, the demoralized—whoever. I didn't take on their way of life. I kept my bearings in Christ—but I entered their world and tried to experience things from their point of view. I've become just about every sort of servant there is in my attempts to lead those I meet into a God-saved life. I did all this because of the Message. I didn't just want to talk about it; I wanted to be in on it!"
[1 Corinthians 9:19-23 The Message]

33

Great Questions

3 GREAT QUESTIONS:

1. **Are you a people pleaser and worried about losing friends?**

    "The man of many friends [a friend of all the world] will prove himself a bad friend, but there is a friend who sticks closer than a brother."
    [Proverbs 18:24 AMP]

2. **Are you prepared to speak the truth in love or do you prefer to kiss butt?**

    "Faithful are the sounds of a friend, but the kisses of an enemy are deceitful."
    [Proverbs 27:6 AMP]

3. **Who in your life sharpens you, chisels you, creates healthy friction in you, in order for you to grow?**

    "As iron sharpens iron, so a friend sharpens a friend."
    [Proverbs 27:17 NLT]

"Successful people ask better questions, and as a result, they get better answers."
- Tony Robbins

34

Happy Home

> "A wise woman builds her home, but a foolish woman tears it down with her own hands."
> [Proverbs 14:1 NLT]

7 HELPFUL RESPONSES [AT HOME]:

1. Being a Buffer (shock absorber)

2. Budgeting (good steward)

3. Breadwinning (contributor)

4. Being Beautiful (inside & out)

5. Being Bountiful (resourceful)

6. Brilliance (problem solver)

7. Building (wise woman)

> "Love begins by taking care of the closest ones – the ones at home."
> - Mother Teresa

7 UNHELPFUL RESPONSES [AT HOME]:

1. Biting (aggressive)
2. Blocking (defensive)
3. Bleeding (emotional train wreck)
4. Ball-breaking (demanding)
5. Being Breakable (fragile)
6. Bullying (intimidator)
7. Badgering (nagging)

> "Love endures long and is patient and kind (at home); love never is envious nor boils over with jealousy, is not boastful or vainglorious, does not display itself haughtily (at home). It is not conceited (arrogant and inflated with pride); it is not rude (unmannerly) and does not act unbecomingly (at home). Love (God's love in us) does not insist on its own rights or its own way (at home), for it is not self-seeking; it is not touchy or fretful or resentful (at home); it takes no account of the evil done to it [it pays no attention to a suffered wrong] (at home). It does not rejoice at injustice and unrighteousness, but rejoices when right and truth prevail (at home). Love bears up under anything and everything that comes (at home), is ever ready to believe the best of every person (at home), its hopes are fadeless under all circumstances, and it endures everything [without weakening] (at home). Love never fails (at home) [never fades out or becomes obsolete or comes to an end]."
> [1 Corinthians 13:4-8 AMP]

35

Heart Condition

**10 THINGS THAT WILL UPSET YOU
IF YOUR HEART IS HEALTHY:**

1. An area not growing. Healthy things grow.

2. People assuming you care because you have to.

3. Not finishing, working hard, but not enough time.

4. Negative talk about leadership or people in general.

5. Wishing you could do more.

6. Someone not meeting their potential.

7. Wasted time.

8. Realizing you let someone down accidentally.

9. Investing, but seeing no results

10. Missing something you should have seen.

"Keep and guard your heart with all vigilance and above all that you guard, for out of it flow the springs of life."
[Proverbs 4:23 AMP]

10 THINGS THAT WILL UPSET YOU IF YOUR HEART IS NOT HEALTHY:

1. People trying to help you.

2. Seeing others advance.

3. Truth.

4. Correction.

5. Holy Spirit conviction.

6. Anyone with authority.

7. Being asked to do anything.

8. God's plan vs. your own plan.

9. Your opinion vs. leadership wisdom.

10. God's timing.

36

Hireling or Son/Daughter

"God's kingdom is like an estate manager who went out early in the morning to hire workers for his vineyard. They agreed on a wage of a dollar a day, and went to work. "Later, about nine o'clock, the manager saw some other men hanging around the town square unemployed. He told them to go to work in his vineyard and he would pay them a fair wage. They went. "He did the same thing at noon, and again at three o'clock. At five o'clock he went back and found still others standing around. He said, 'Why are you standing around all day doing nothing?' "They said, 'Because no one hired us.' "He told them to go to work in his vineyard. "When the day's work was over, the owner of the vineyard instructed his foreman, 'Call the workers in and pay them their wages. Start with the last hired and go on to the first.' "Those hired at five o'clock came up and were each given a dollar. When those who were hired first saw that, they assumed they would get far more. But they got the same, each of them one dollar. Taking the dollar, they groused angrily to the manager, 'These last workers put in only one easy hour, and you just made them equal to us, who slaved all day under a scorching sun.' "He replied to the one speaking for the rest, 'Friend, I haven't been unfair. We agreed on the wage of a dollar, didn't we? So take it and go. I decided to give to the one who came last the same as you. Can't I do what I want with my own money? Are you going to get stingy because I am generous?'"

[Matthew 20:1-15 The Message]

10 DIFFERENCES BETWEEN BEING A HIRELING AND BEING A SON OR DAUGHTER:

1. A hireling works to advance themselves.
   A son or daughter works to advance the whole family (kingdom).

2. A hireling earns a reward.
   A son or daughter reaps a reward.

3. A hireling works for a fair wage.
   A son or daughter works because they know the price that's been paid for them.

4. A hireling waits to be called.
   A son or daughter sees a need and fills it.

5. A hireling works with a clock in-clock out system.
   A son or daughter works with an eternal clock system.

6. A hireling may work for a season.
   A son or daughter works for a lifetime.

7. A hireling will never feel like they belong.
   A son or daughter knows they are home.

8. While a hireling keeps record of their work.
   A son or daughter works to be fruitful.

9. A hireling does what it's told.
   A son or daughter are one step ahead.

10. A hireling works for a living,
    A son or daughter works because it is life giving.

37

Home Beautiful Essentials

1. Value what you have.

2. Clean as you go - simple.

3. Be ready for anything.

4. Lighting - lighting attracts and welcomes.

5. Scents - candles or food, scents create memories.

6. Laundry is not an event. Be thankful you have clothes to wash.

7. Build a routine, for sanity's sake. But don't be hard on yourself if something is missed.

8. Always have something to offer, even if it is just tea. It opens doors (and it's inexpensive).

9. Let your home be 'lived in'. People don't want to feel like they can't take their shoes off and relax.

10. Love where you live. Even if it's seasonal, you have a home.

"Never lose an opportunity of seeing anything beautiful, for beauty is God's handwriting."
- Ralph Waldo Emerson

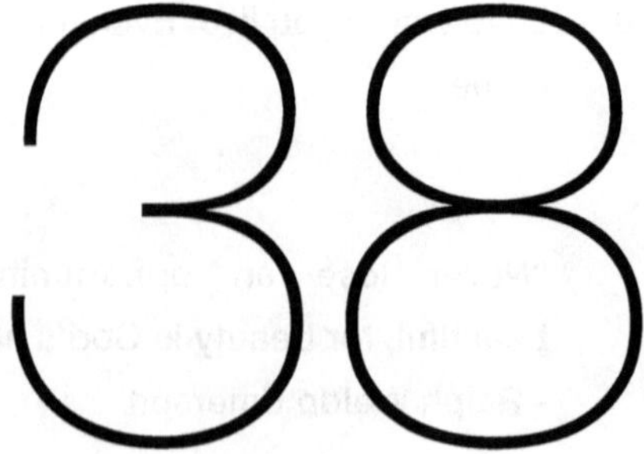

Honor Code

Christian leaders have a responsibility to develop and exhibit mature Christian behavior. This should be the basic premise of our desire to lead others. While serving as a leader we should commit to present a good appearance at all times. In both behavior and attire, we should strive to demonstrate Biblical standards in all situations.

As Christian leaders, the way we present ourselves to others is of vital importance to the way others perceive Jesus. Our conduct should never be an embarrassment to Jesus, but should exemplify the best qualities of a mature believer and servant leader. Exemplifying the highest moral commitment, great leaders maintain a disciplined life of Church attendance, Bible reading, prayer, discipleship and giving. By providing an example in speech and action, we encourage others to grow in Christ and become servant leaders themselves. Great leaders regard this way of life as an essential part of their growth and development, not as an imposition or restriction.

Remember: spiritual maturity isn't based on how long we've known God. Spiritual maturity is based on how long we've trusted and obeyed Him.

IT'S TIME to lead with our lives!

> "You can develop a healthy, robust community that lives right with God and enjoy its results only if you do the hard work of getting along with each other, treating each other with dignity ad honor."
>
> [James 3:18 The Message]

WHAT HONOR IS:

1. Uncompromising honesty.
2. Trustworthiness.
3. Unquestioned integrity.
4. Sincerity.
5. Strong adherence to truth.
6. Highest moral principles.
7. Absence of deceit or fraud.
8. Strict conformity to what is morally right.
9. Consideration of others.
10. Distinct loyalty.

"Ability without honor is useless."
- Marcus Tullius Cicero

WHO WE SHOULD HONOR:

> **"Honor God with everything you own; give him the first and the best."**
> **[Proverbs 3:9 The Message]**

1. God

2. Parents

3. Children

4. Spouse

5. Others

6. Leaders

7. All people

> **"Honor all people. Love the brotherhood. Fear God. Honor the king."**
> **[1 Peter 2:16 AMP]**

10 WAYS TO HONOR YOUR LEADERS

> "Obey your spiritual leaders, and do what they say. Their work is to watch over your souls, and they are accountable to God. Give them reason to do this with joy and not with sorrow. That would certainly not be for your benefit."
> [Hebrews 13:17 NLT]

1. Follow them.

2. Speak positively about them.

3. Trust them.

4. Write a thank you card.

5. Support their vision

6. Speak respectfully to them.

7. Value their time.

8. Pray for them.

9. Believe in them.

10. Serve them.

> "Success without honor is an unseasoned dish; it will satisfy your hunger, but it won't taste good."
> - Joe Paterno

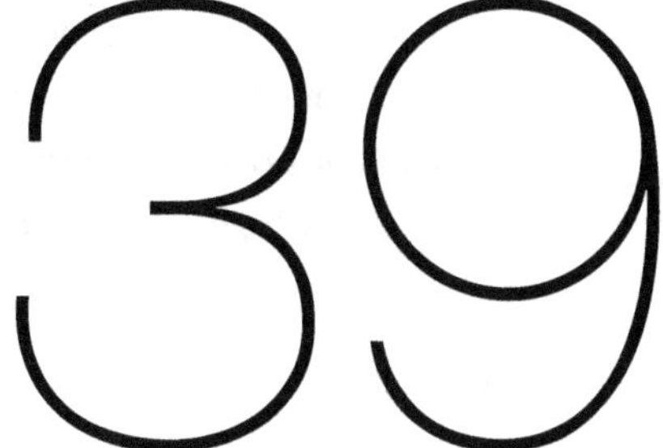

How to Build a High Completion Drive

1. Set your alarm 15 minutes earlier. You will be surprised at how much you can get done.

2. Make a To-Do List. Checking things off is rewarding and encouraging.

3. Try and do tomorrow's work today, if possible.

4. Have and use a calendar. It will help you stay organized.

5. Own what you do. It's all up to you. Be proud of it.

6. Set an atmosphere if possible. Whether it be a candle, favorite music, or even a picture of someone you love.

7. Sleep. Be responsible.

8. Remember you get better as you do something more. Always be looking at ways to maximize what you do, and how you do it.

9. Learn the tricks. Reading the instructions of devices can let you know how to get everything out of what you have. Example: Cell phone calendars, how to set an alarm every month without having to do each manually. Work smarter, not harder.

10. Remember why you do what you do.

40

IMAGINE

"God can do anything, you know—far more than you could ever imagine or guess or request in your wildest dreams! He does it not by pushing us around but by working within us, his Spirit deeply and gently within us."
[Ephesians 3:20-22 The Message]

10 COMPELLING REASONS TO COME TO IMAGINE:

1. COME to discover purpose.
2. COME to be inspired.
3. COME to give
4. COME to belong.
5. COME to worship
6. COME to receive.
7. COME to participate
8. COME to follow.
9. COME to dream.
10. COME to Jesus.

41

Lady Liberty

> "Listen carefully: Unless a grain of wheat is buried in the ground, dead to the world, it is never any more than a grain of wheat. But if it is buried, it sprouts and reproduces itself many times over. In the same way, anyone who holds on to life just as it is destroys that life. But if you let it go, reckless in your love, you'll have it forever, real and eternal. "If any of you wants to serve me, then follow me. Then you'll be where I am, ready to serve at a moment's notice. The Father will honor and reward anyone who serves me.
> [John 12:25-26 The Message]

There is a line between leadership and taking liberty, and we need know where it is so we don't fall into the trap of crossing over it.

> "The Lord is my chosen and assigned portion, my cup; You hold and maintain my lot. The lines have fallen for me in pleasant places; yes, I have a good heritage. I will bless the Lord, Who has given me counsel; yes, my heart instructs me in the night seasons."
> [Psalm 16:5-7 AMP]

Perhaps you have had some 'unpleasant' experiences in your leadership journey so far. Could it be that you may have 'crossed a line' that you shouldn't have crossed? Perhaps you have had an unpleasant experience because you exercised 'liberty' over 'discretion'. It could be that you crossed the line between leadership and liberty.

LIBERTY:

Freedom from: control, interference, obligation, restriction; right to do, think, speak, according to personal choice.

DISCRETION:

The power or right to decide or act according to one's own judgment; freedom of judgment or choice:

The marked difference between leadership and liberty is the use of personal freedom, and whether we have it or not. As leaders we are free to exercise our will. But as leaders we understand and value discretion over personal liberty.

DIFFERENCES BETWEEN LEADERSHIP & LIBERTY:

1. Leadership
   Follows leadership.
   Liberty
   Follows anyone or anything it wants to.

2. Leadership
   Knows there's lots to learn.
   Liberty
   Seems to know it all.

3. Leadership
   Promotes others.
   Liberty
   Promotes itself.

4. Leadership
   Has longevity and lasts the distance.
   Liberty
   Leaves at will, and usually too soon.

5. **Leadership**

   Thinks first & speaks if necessary.

   Liberty

   Speaks first and does it all too often.

6. **Leadership**

   Confronts in love.

   Liberty

   Confronts in defense.

7. **Leadership**

   Gives because it trusts.

   Liberty

   Withholds because it can.

8. **Leadership**

   Uses discretion.

   Liberty

   Uses people.

9. **Leadership**

   Is loyal.

   Liberty

   Is limited.

10. **Leadership**

    Lives by Biblical pattern.

    Liberty

    Lives by personal agenda.

11. **Leadership**

    Lends, shares and gives.

    Liberty

    Begs, borrows and steals.

12. Leadership
    Forgives and forgets.
    Liberty
    Forgets to forgive.

13. Leadership
    Accepts responsibility.
    Liberty
    Objects to being accountable.

14. Leadership
    Has desires and yet defers.
    Liberty
    Has cravings and satisfies them.

15. Leadership
    Is rewarded by God and others.
    Liberty
    Rewards itself.

16. Leadership
    Yields.
    Liberty
    Proceeds.

17. Leadership
    Contributes.
    Liberty
    Consumes.

> "Obey your spiritual leaders, and do what they say. Their work is to watch over your souls, and they are accountable to God. Give them reason to do this with joy and not with sorrow. That would certainly not be for your benefit."
> [Hebrews 13:17 NLT]

42

Last Great Words

"Paul's Final Greetings
"Dear brothers and sisters, I close my letter with these last words: Rejoice. Change your ways. Encourage each other. Live in harmony and peace. Then the God of love and peace will be with you."
[2 Corinthians 13:11 NLT]

5 LAST GREAT WORDS:

1. Rejoice.
   Praise Him.

2. Change your ways.
   Follow Him.

3. Encourage each other.
   Exemplify Him.

4. Live in harmony and peace.
   Please Him.

5. THEN the God of love and peace will be with you.
   Enjoy Him!

43

Leadership Friendships

Blog by Pastor Kerri Weems - Celebration Church

Can a Pastor's Wife Have Friends?

"Can a pastor's wife have friends that are in her congregation? On staff? When we planted our church, we moved from the relatively small town of Baton Rouge, where both Stovall and I grew up, to the larger city of Jacksonville. In Baton Rouge I had a lifetime of shared history with a close-knit group of friends, but in Jacksonville we knew no one. I had no choice but to be friends with people in my congregation and on our staff – and they turned out to be really fun and life-giving friendships. Here are a few tips I learned along the way that might help you out:

1. Start off being just who you are.
   You can't sustain what is not authentic. If you're outgoing and exuberant, then use that gift. If you are serious and reserved, then use the gifts that come with that package. When you try to be someone you're not, you set unrealistic expectations for the future, and you set yourself up for frustration.

2. Embrace your role as spiritual leader.
   There is so much emphasis on transparency today that sometimes I think we forget that we are called to maturity, not merely authenticity. Yes, your congregants and staff members want you to be authentic, but they also want you to be an example of spiritual maturity. Hello... that's probably why they want to get close to you. Live a life of integrity and this won't be a problem for you.

3. **Choose carefully.**
   Just because you can be friends with everybody doesn't mean you should. This is a really fuzzy boundary for Pastor's Wives, because we are called to ministry for people. It seems counter intuitive not to allow everybody into our intimate circle. Remember this, even Jesus, although he had hundreds of disciples, only had 12 close friends his entire ministry. And even within those 12, there were three with whom he was particularly close. I know there is a typological explanation behind that observation, but there is also an example to us that we can teach and lead people without necessarily being in intimate friendship with them.

4. **Go slowly.**
   We can feel so lonely when we start off in a church plant or new church that we can foolishly try to escalate the intimacy level of these new friendships beyond what they are ready to bear. It is hard to start over making friends when you left a lifetime of deep friendships behind at home. The new ones you are making feel shallow and a bit awkward by comparison. But give them time to flourish at their own pace. Friendships that are God-breathed deepen and grow – it's a simple as that!

You know, I think we give people less credit than they deserve sometimes. I think people can handle a lot more of our "humanity" than we leaders think they can. People appreciate authenticity and maturity. They know you have struggles and frustrations just like them, and when they see you navigate your "stuff" and grow in maturity, they grow in respect for you as well."

44

Leadership Observations

1. **Leaders live it.**
   What you say, you live – by example.

2. **Leaders tune into it.**
   You are in touch with the reality of those you lead.

3. **Leaders direct with precision.**
   Followers admire your clear and precise direction. You know where you're going which makes you easy to follow!

4. **Leaders notice everything.**
   You value people most of all and your attention to detail is greatly admired. You notice everything and you chose when the right time to say something and when not to is.

5. **Leaders choose their battles.**
   You are always thinking about the best for others, you value people future. You pick what battles are worth fighting.

6. **Leaders value their families.**
   You value your family. You work hard, but know when to have fun. You are committed.

7. **Leaders are creative.**
   You are creative. You are always thinking how something could be done better.

8. **Leaders value what God values.**
   You are always seeking what He has eyes to see.

9. Leaders lead by perspective not power.
You have a perspective in life that allows you to lead with your heart. But you are just as impacting and respected as any leader who leads with their power.

10. Leaders draw the best out of followers.
You have the best interest in mind for all areas of your team's lives not just the areas that may help you. And your followers fully trust you because of that. Your leadership draws the potential out in people who can't see it for themselves.

11. Leaders explain with clarity.
Your leadership is clear and intentional. You always explain the 'why' behind the 'what' along with the 'way'. Your leadership makes my small become really big because you lead us to build together.

12. Leaders lead with grace.
Your leadership is always covered in grace and taught from what the Bible says so is not contradicting to God's Word.

13. Leaders lead with wisdom.
You are good at playing the movie out and making smart, effective decisions. You always have something wise to say in a situation.

14. Leaders are organized.
You are very good at getting things organized for events or days and logistically making things happen, and organizing a big group of people to do things!

15. **Leaders correct by redirect.**
You are direct but in an incredibly loving way. You never tell people that they're wrong and make them feel that they're not capable. You show a different way while affirming the person and the job that they've done.

16. **Leaders challenge by encouragement.**
You have the ability to challenge people without sending them into a mental and emotional break-down. Even when you are challenging, you are very encouraging. You are real and honest and share openly that you are still learning and growing and that you have not yet 'arrived'!

17. **Leaders dream a bigger dream.**
As our lives grow as leaders, so too do our dreams. Our dreams grow not just for ourselves but for others. Within every leader's dream is the dream of the people following them. It is our responsibility to continually dream a bigger dream!

"Pattern yourselves after me [follow my example], as I imitate and follow Christ (the Messiah)."
[1 Corinthians 11:1 AMP]

45

Leadership Thoughts From Solomon

> "As dead flies cause even a bottle of perfume to stink, so a little foolishness spoils great wisdom and honor. A wise person chooses the right road; a fool takes the wrong one. You can identify fools just by the way they walk down the street! If your boss is angry at you, don't quit! A quiet spirit can overcome even great mistakes... Using a dull ax requires great strength, so sharpen the blade. That's the value of wisdom; it helps you succeed... A party gives laughter, wine gives happiness, and money gives everything! Never make light of the king, even in your thoughts. And don't make fun of the powerful, even in your own bedroom. For a little bird might deliver your message and tell them what you said.
> [Ecclesiastes 10:1-20 NLT]

7 THINGS TO THINK ABOUT:

1. Dead flies.

2. A lonely road.

3. The way we walk.

4. An angry boss.

5. A dull axe.

6. Money.

7. A little bird.

1. Dead Flies

"As dead flies cause even a bottle of perfume to stink, so a little foolishness spoils great wisdom and honor."
[Ecclesiastes 10:1 NLT]

- What is a little foolishness?
- Why does it matter?

2. A Lonely Road

"A wise person chooses the right road; a fool takes the wrong one."
[Ecclesiastes 10:2 NLT]

- Do most people live with regret?
- Why?

3. The Way We Walk

"You can identify fools just by the way they walk down the street!"
[Ecclesiastes 10:3 NLT]

- What is your demeanor (body language) like?
- What does it say about you?

4. An Angry Boss

"If your boss is angry at you, don't quit! A quiet spirit can overcome even great mistakes."
[Ecclesiastes 10:4 NLT]

- What do you want to quit right now?
- How do you overcome the urge to quit?

5. A Dull Axe

"Using a dull ax requires great strength, so sharpen the blade. That's the value of wisdom; it helps you succeed."
[Ecclesiastes 10:10 NLT]

- What is wearing you out?
- Who are you spending time with to sharpen you?

6. Money

"A party gives laughter, wine gives happiness, and money gives everything!"
[Ecclesiastes 10:19 NLT]

- Why does finance cause stress?
- How is your budget going?

7. A Little Bird

"Never make light of the king, even in your thoughts. And don't make fun of the powerful, even in your own bedroom. For a little bird might deliver your message and tell them what you said."
[Ecclesiastes 10:20 NLT]

- Honor starts and finishes in the heart.
- Honor starts and finishes at home.
- What is in your heart will come out of your mouth.
- What would the little birdie repeat from you lately?

46

Leadership Values

1. Character
   1 Corinthians 6:12

2. "Count me in"
   Mark 2:1-12

3. Generosity
   2 Corinthians 9:6

4. 2nd Mile
   Matthew 5:38-42

5. Accountability
   Proverbs 15:31

6. Loyalty
   Ruth 1:16-18

7. Encouragement
   Proverbs 3:27

8. Kingdom First
   Matthew 6:33

9. Growing Capacity
   Matthew 13:23

10. Honesty
    Proverbs 24:26

47

Let Love Rule

Love is the President.

PRESIDE:
To hold the position of authority; act as chairperson or president. To possess or exercise authority or control.

> "God presides over heaven's court; he pronounces judgment on the heavenly beings: How long will you hand down unjust decisions by favoring the wicked? Give justice to the poor and the orphan; uphold the rights of the oppressed and the destitute."
> [Psalm 82:1-3 NLT]

"God stands, as chief director...We must not forget that God stands amongst us... To do unjustly is bad, but to judge unjustly is much worse, because it is doing wrong under color of right..." Matthew Henry's Commentary

WHAT HAPPENS WHEN LOVE PRESIDES?

1. I win, you win [no-one loses].

> "You may have to draw straws when faced with a tough decision. Do a favor and win a friend forever; nothing can untie that bond."
> [Proverbs 18:18-19 The Message]

2. Everyone gets to start again [a blank canvas].

"So if you're serious about living this new resurrection life with Christ, act like it. Pursue the things over which Christ presides. Don't shuffle along, eyes to the ground, absorbed with the things right in front of you. Look up, and be alert to what is going on around Christ that's where the action is. See things from his perspective. Your old life is dead. Your new life, which is your real life even though invisible to spectators is with Christ in God. He is your life. When Christ (your real life, remember) shows up again on this earth, you'll show up, too the real you, the glorious you. Meanwhile, be content with obscurity, like Christ."
[Colossians 3:1-4 The Message]

3. Love resides [literally takes up residency].

RESIDENT:
One who lives in a place permanently or for an extended period.

"I give you a new commandment: that you should love one another. Just as I have loved you, so you too should love one another. By this shall all [men] know that you are My disciples, if you love one another [if you keep on showing love among yourselves]."
[John 13:34-35 AMP]

IT'S TIME TO LOVE, LOVE, LOVE!

"The reputation of their profession [John 13:35]: By this shall all men know that you are my disciples, if you have love one to another. Observe, We must have love, not only show love, but have it in the root and habit of it, and have it when there is not any present occasion to show it; have it ready. "Hereby it will appear that you are indeed my followers by following me in this." Note, Brotherly love is the badge of Christ's disciples. By this he knows them, by this they may know themselves [1 John 2:14], and by this others may know them. This is the livery of his family, the distinguishing character of his disciples; this he would have them noted for, as that wherein they excelled all others—their loving one another. This was what their Master was famous for; all that ever heard of him have heard of his love, his great love; and therefore, if you see any people more affectionate one to another than what is common, say, "Certainly these are the followers of Christ, they have been with Jesus." - Matthew Henry's Commentary

48

Lighten Up!

Here's one of those funny emails a friend sent my way. It's good to remember we all need a good laugh, and often!

THE NEXT SURVIVOR SERIES
RULES OF ENGAGEMENT:

1. Six married men will be dropped on an island with one car and 3 kids each for six weeks.

2. Each kid will play two sports and either take music or dance classes.

3. There is no fast food.

4. Each man must take care of his 3 kids; keep his assigned house clean, correct all homework, and complete science projects, cook, do laundry, and pay a list of 'pretend' bills with not enough money.

5. In addition, each man will have to budget in money for groceries each week.

6. Each man must remember the birthdays of all their friends and relatives, and send cards out on time - no emailing.

7. Each man must also take each child to a doctor's appointment, a dentist appointment and a haircut appointment.

8. A test will be given at the end of the six weeks, and each father will be required to know all of the following information:

    - Each child's birthday
    - Height
    - Weight
    - Shoe size
    - Clothes size
    - Doctor's name.

    Also the child's:

    - Weight at birth
    - Length at birth
    - Time of birth
    - Length of labor

    Each child's:

    - Favorite color
    - Middle name
    - Favorite snack

- Favorite song
- Favorite drink
- Favorite toy
- Biggest fear
- And what they want to be when they grow up...

9. All the above must be completed while working in either full time (preferably) or part time employment to assist in the financial input for the family.

10. The kids vote them off the island based on performance. The last man wins only if..... he still has enough energy to be intimate with his spouse at a moment's notice.

11. If the last man does win, he can play the game over and over and over again for the next 18-25 years eventually earning the right to be called Mom!

12. After you get done laughing, read this to as many women as you think will get a laugh out of it and as many men as you think can handle it!

"I'll convert their weeping into laughter, lavishing comfort, invading their grief with joy. "
[Jeremiah 31:10 The Message]

49

Little Creepers

"You were running superbly! Who cut in on you, deflecting you from the true course of obedience? This detour doesn't come from the One who called you into the race in the first place. And please don't toss this off as insignificant. It only takes a minute amount of yeast, you know, to permeate an entire loaf of bread. Deep down, the Master has given me confidence that you will not defect. But the one who is upsetting you, whoever he is, will bear the divine judgment."
[Galatians 5:7-10 The Message]

10 LITTLE CREEPERS:

1. Thinking
(double-minded confusion)

2. Familiarity
(presumption road)

3. Lethargy
(tired and heavy body & soul)

4. Worry
(anxiety that rules the roost)

5. Pride
(always goes before a big fat fall)

6. Friends
[the good the bad the ugly]

7. Self
(me, myself, I)

8. Lack
(never having enough)

9. Avoidance
(burying your head in the sand)

10. Desperation
(desperately wanting to date)

"Dear friend, guard Clear Thinking and Common Sense with your life; don't for a minute lose sight of them. They'll keep your soul alive and well, they'll keep you fit and attractive. You'll travel safely, you'll neither tire nor trip. You'll take afternoon naps without a worry, you'll enjoy a good night's sleep."
[Proverbs 3:21 The Message]

50

Little Miss

> "My old self has been crucified with Christ. It is no longer I who live, but Christ lives in me. So I live in this earthly body by trusting in the Son of God, who loved me and gave himself for me."
> [Galatians 2:20 NLT]

Maybe IT'S TIME to grow up and out of our 'Little Miss' season. Just wondering!

1. Miss-Understood

    Fact: To take (words, statements, etc.) in a wrong sense; to understand wrongly; to fail to understand or interpret rightly the words or behavior of a person.

    Truth: Take responsibility for you and don't co-sign accusation.

2. Miss-Represented

    Fact: To give an incorrect or misleading representation of a person or situation.

    Truth: 'Shutteth uppeth' and allow God to shed light and bring justice.

3. Miss-Treated

    Fact: To treat badly or incorrectly.

    Truth: Renew your mind and learn to toughen up a little.

4. Miss-Demeanor

Fact: A minor crime, usually dealt with informally by a fine rather than jail. It is of no big deal or major consequence.

Truth: We need to deal with sin [hypocrisy] properly or sin will deal with us.

5. Miss-Independence

Fact: Freedom from the advice, influence, support, aid, or the like, of others.

Truth: It is wise to submit your life to Biblical authority.

> "Get all the advice and instruction you can, so you will be wise the rest of your life. You can make many plans, but the LORD's purpose will prevail."
> [Proverbs 19:20-21 NLT]

Perhaps you were raised to be 'Little Miss Independence'. There's a big difference between 'personal responsibility' and 'independence.' Getting a job and paying bills is 'personal responsibility'. Making decisions based on what the Bible says is maturity!

Maybe you'll feel like you been a 'Little Miss-Taken' or a 'Little Taken Advantage Of'. Remember – no-one can take away from you what you freely give. Don't fall for 'buyers remorse' syndrome. When you sow your time, talent and treasure, there's no such thing as 'sower's remorse'.

6. Miss-Fit

Fact: One who is unable to adjust to one's environment or circumstances or is considered to be disturbingly different from others.
Truth: Timing is everything.

> "He has made everything beautiful in its time. He also has planted eternity in men's hearts and minds [a divinely implanted sense of a purpose working through the ages which nothing under the sun but God alone can satisfy], yet so that men cannot find out what God has done from the beginning to the end."
> [Ecclesiastes 3:11 AMP]

Perhaps you feel like you're a 'Little Miss-Fit'. There is a God shaped void in all of us that only God Himself can satisfy. This void is filled by God's presence. His timing makes our lives beautiful if we stay the distance. Maybe you feel as though your life is in a season of 'observation' right now, where you feel that you aren't really doing anything. Trust me! Watching, observing, learning, gleaning will change your life, and will help to shape your future leadership.

7. Miss-Conception

Fact: A mistaken thought, idea or notion.
Truth: Allow the Bible to become your personal belief system.

"Do not be conformed to this world (this age), [fashioned after and adapted to its external, superficial customs], but be transformed (changed) by the [entire] renewal of your mind [by its new ideals and its new attitude], so that you may prove [for yourselves] what is the good and acceptable and perfect will of God, even the thing which is good and acceptable and perfect [in His sight for you]."
[Romans 12:2 AMP]

If you are 'Little Miss-Conception' your belief system is different from that the Bible says. IT'S TIME to simplify and solidify your beliefs so that you can lose the complicated thought processes and adopt Biblical principles to think and live by.

8. Miss-Opportunity

Fact: Opportunity can be a good position, chance, or prospect, as for advancement or success. It can be a favorable or advantageous circumstance or combination of circumstances.

Truth: Drawing near opens doors of opportunity.

"Therefore submit to God. Resist the devil and he will flee from you. Draw near to God and He will draw near to you..."
[James 4:7-8 NKJV]

We need to make room in our lives physically, mentally and spiritually. We need to step up. We need to allow our hearts to be excavated by the Holy Spirit, and we need to focus our thinking, so we will be ready for opportunity that's coming our way. Leadership requires us to position ourselves. If you stand to the side of an automatic door it won't open for you. You need to stand in the right place at the right time for the sensor to be triggered to open the door. Where have you positioned yourself?

9. Miss-Guilty

Fact: When we know right and live wrong we will feel guilty and confused.

Truth: We can live free of all guilt and confusion when we live our lives set apart [different] – not the same...

> "For everyone has sinned; we all fall short of God's glorious standard. Yet God, with undeserved kindness, declares that we are righteous. He did this through Christ Jesus when he freed us from the penalty for our sins. For God presented Jesus as the sacrifice for sin. People are made right with God when they believe that Jesus sacrificed his life, shedding his blood. This sacrifice shows that God was being fair when he held back and did not punish those who sinned in times past, for he was looking ahead and including them in what he would do in this present time. God did this to demonstrate his righteousness, for he himself is fair and just, and he declares sinners to be right in his sight when they believe in Jesus."
> [Romans 3:23-26 NLT]

10. Miss-Informed

Fact: "No-one told me."
"I was taught something that wasn't true."
"I didn't know."

Truth: BIBLE SAYS

> "Let each generation tell its children of your mighty acts; let them proclaim your power."
> [Psalm 145:4 NLT]

When we place a person or a dream or a thing or a problem, or a circumstance above Jesus in our lives, we establish an idol. An Idol is an image used as an object of worship. It is a false god. It is something visible but without substance.

Does your life speak of the mighty acts and power of God, or does your life speak of the mighty big dreams and mighty powerful problems you have?

> "Maturity is achieved when a person postpones immediate pleasures for long-term values."
> - Joshua L. Liebman

Perhaps IT'S TIME to grow up Little Miss!

51

Little Things That Are A Big Deal

1. How you respond.
   You can instantly read the signs of a leader with a stinky attitude, because of how they respond.

2. Who you surround yourself with.
   Familiarity breeds contempt.

3. How you read your Bible.
   Reading it isn't enough. Believing and doing is another level.

4. Other people's time.
   Time is valuable; don't keep people waiting on you.

5. Who/what you search for when things get tough.
   Calling on someone who doesn't understand the culture you work in won't be able to help you.

6. Twitter.
   Think before you tweet. People are following you and to them they think you represent our church, because of your leadership.

7. How you spend your money.
   If you can't afford to invest in the organization of which you are a leader, but you continue to spend money on personal entertainment - where are your priorities?

8. How you spend your down time.
   Everything is permissible, but not everything is profitable.

9. Your perspective.
   We always need to ensure that our perspective reflects that of God's perspective and our leaders' perspective, whilst forming our own perspective. Eternity should always be our perspective.

10. How you deliver or relay a message to people following you.
    You can be destructive if you fail to help explain the why behind the what.

"Management is doing things right; leadership is doing the right things."
- Peter Drucker

52

Loving Ministry and Building God's Church

> "And I tell you that you are Peter, and on this rock I will build my church, and the gates of Hades will not overcome it."
> [Matthew 16:18 NIV]

10 REASONS WHY WE SHOULD LOVE MINISTRY AND BUILDING GOD'S CHURCH:

1. To be like Jesus.
   The Bible says Jesus came to build his church, and that the gates of hell will not prevail against it. If we want to be like Jesus, we will want to build His church. The Holy Spirit came when they were all gathered in one place.

2. To please God.
   I want to please God. 1 John 2:3 says that we love Him by obeying his commands. So I will build His church, for faith without deeds is dead.

3. To find destiny.
   We find destiny and hope for our own lives in church, so the least we can do, is build His church for others.

4. To pool resource.
   My resource can go so far, until it's combined with the resource of the rest of the body's. That's an example of the church being the answer. We can be part of someone else's miracle.

5. To be fully functional.
   The church is the body of Christ. As leaders, we need to be functional parts of the body. Without my contribution, I'm making some part of the body dysfunctional. We are the family of God and it's our privilege and responsibility to do our part.

6. To worship.
   My voice is helpful, but joined in unity with hundreds of others. That's when walls break down. The shout of a united community of people broke down the walls of Jericho. Worship is great alone, in the privacy of your room, but when we worship together in the House of God, there is unity, and where there is unity, God commands a blessing.

7. To love people.
   People matter. People matter to God and people should matter to us. In good times and tough times, families are designed to stick together. And a healthy church is more than a healthy community – it's a family. We need to remember to love God, love people, and love life in every season.

8. To flourish.
   The Bible talks about trusting your leaders. Without being in a healthy church, who are you following? It is because of being planted in a healthy church and following great leaders that I am able to lead others today. When I am planted, then I will flourish.

9. To see people healed, whole and set free.
   Jesus was a kids pastor and a youth leader. He cared for the broken, the widow, the orphan, the sick, the outcast, the sinner and the saint, and I want to be like Jesus. We can follow His example and build His church - His community. Jesus healed people wherever He went. Great crowds grew around Him as he saw need and healed multitudes. We are called to see people healed and whole, set free to live a free life in Christ.

10. To be in the presence of God.
    Where two or more are gathered in His name, there he is amongst them. I want to be where the presence of God is always.

"You can be committed to the Church but not committed to Christ, but you cannot be committed to Christ and not committed to church."
– Joel Osteen

53

Loyal Heart - Loyal Life

LOYAL HEART = LOYAL LIFE

1. Humble heart
   Humble life

2. Open heart
   Open life

3. Immovable heart
   Immovable life

4. Uncompromised heart
   Uncompromised life

5. Renewed heart
   Renewed life

6. Committed heart
   Committed life

7. A heart that knows God
   Godly life

> "For every tree is known by its own fruit. For men do not gather figs from thorns, nor do they gather grapes from a bramble bush. A good man out of the good treasure of his heart brings forth good; and an evil man out of the evil treasure of his heart brings forth evil. For out of the abundance of the heart his mouth [and his life!] speaks."
> [Luke 6:44-46 NKJV]

DISLOYAL HEART = DISLOYAL LIFE

1. Bad attitude.
2. Entitlement.
3. Uncommitted
4. Inconsistent.
5. Selfishness.
6. Someone causes others to feel violated.
7. Unfaithful
8. Unpredictable.
9. Sneaky.
10. Unstable.

> "An ounce of loyalty is worth a pound of cleverness."
> - Elbert Hubbard

LOYAL REFLECTIONS

1. A LOYAL CONVICTION
(reflects a heart that's humble)

It is sometimes, for some people, somehow easier to be loyal to God and not give a second thought to the people God has put in their lives. We ought to love God yes. His Word says we also ought to love people. Loyalty to another human being will always cost us. Love is costly! True love shines brightly in the heart of a loyal soul.

"Never let loyalty and kindness leave you! Tie them around your neck as a reminder. Write them deep within your heart. Then you will find favor with both God and people, and you will earn a good reputation."
[Proverbs 3:3-4 NLT]

2. A LOYAL PURPOSE
(reflects a heart that's open)

We are encouraged at the beginning of a New Year to plan our lives out. Yes, good planning is very important. But always remember that your primary plan should be to make room for God's plan... It's most unhelpful to your life to plan yourself into a competition with GOD!

"You can make many plans, but the Lord's purpose will prevail. Loyalty makes a person attractive."
[Proverbs 19:21 NLT]

3. A LOYAL FAITH
(reflects a heart that's immovable)

There are some things that are just non-negotiable. We somehow equate our doubting immaturity with it being some kind of spiritual flexibility. It isn't. Our faith in our God needs to be immovable – set in stone!

"If you need wisdom, ask our generous God, and he will give it to you. He will not rebuke you for asking. But when you ask him, be sure that your faith is in God alone. Do not waver, for a person with divided loyalty is as unsettled as a wave of the sea that is blown and tossed by the wind. Such people should not expect to receive anything from the Lord. Their loyalty is divided between God and the world, and they are unstable in everything they do."
[James 1:5-9 New Living Translation]

4. A LOYAL LIFE
(reflects a heart that's uncompromised)

We can do all the right things but with the wrong heart. We can make all the right noises but be devoid of care. If you know right and do wrong long enough it becomes a lifestyle.

"Amaziah was twenty-five years old when he became king, and he reigned twenty-nine years in Jerusalem. His mother's name was Jehoaddan of Jerusalem. And he did what was right in the sight of the LORD, but not with a loyal heart."
[2 Chronicles 25:1-2 NKJV]

5. A LOYAL SPIRIT
(reflects a heart that's renewed)

If God doesn't renew our heart we will have a skeptical spirit. Our heart needs a deep cleanse every day. If not, life's impurities will fester and our spirit will be affected.

"Create in me a clean heart, O God. Renew a loyal spirit within me."
[Psalm 51:10 NLT]

6. A LOYAL FOREVER
(reflects a heart that's committed)

How long is forever? How long is a piece of string? How long a person is happy? Until someone gets what they want? Our God is loyal always and ever!

"Enter with the password: "Thank you!" Make yourselves at home, talking praise. Thank him. Worship him. For God is sheer beauty, all-generous in love, loyal always and ever."
[Psalm 100:4-5 The Message]

7. A LOYAL GOD
(reflects a heart that knows God)

Do not limit a limitless God! He is not like you and me. He is not like the most wonderful person you know. He is GOD and He can handle our anything! We will always doubt his loyalty to us if we don't truly know who He is.

"God's love is meteoric, His loyalty astronomic, His purpose titanic, His verdicts oceanic. Yet in His largeness nothing gets lost; not a man, not a mouse, slips through the cracks."
Psalm 36:5 (The Message)

54

Loyalty vs Faithfulness

Loyal: Latin word meaning: legal or binding.
Faithful: meaning: true to the facts.

1. Faithfulness Is attached to a project
   Loyalty Is attached to a person

2. Faithfulness can operate in offence
   Loyalty cannot be offended

3. Faithfulness is transferrable
   Loyalty cannot be bought

4. Faithfulness Is reflected in our hands
   Loyalty is reflected in our heart

5. Faithfulness can be circumstantial and seasonal
   Loyalty is crystal clear and unchanging

6. Faithfulness loves to serve
   Loyalty serves to love

7. You can be faithful but disloyal
   You cannot be loyal and unfaithful

"Many a man proclaims his own loyalty, but who can find a trustworthy man?"
[Proverbs 20:6 NASB]

55

Making Bank

> "Remember this—a farmer who plants only a few seeds will get a small crop. But the one who plants generously will get a generous crop. You must each decide in your heart how much to give. And don't give reluctantly or in response to pressure. "For God loves a person who gives cheerfully." And God will generously provide all you need. Then you will always have everything you need and plenty left over to share with others. As the Scriptures say, "They share freely and give generously to the poor. Their good deeds will be remembered forever." For God is the one who provides seed for the farmer and then bread to eat. In the same way, he will provide and increase your resources and then produce a great harvest of generosity in you. Yes, you will be enriched in every way so that you can always be generous. And when we take your gifts to those who need them, they will thank God."
> [2 Corinthians 9:6-11 NLT]

7 GREAT REASONS TO MAKE BANK:

1. To provide for your family.
2. To live comfortably without financial worry.
3. To leave a legacy behind.
4. To inspire others to build the Kingdom of God.
5. To finance the Vision of the Church.
6. To be the solution to multitudes of problems.
7. To be able to buy whatever you want for others.

56

Marks of a Great Leader

1. INTEGRITY

    - Moral courage; conviction with longevity.
    - Willingness to stick to ones beliefs.
    - Ability to pursue a course of action in the face of adversity.
    - Literally: knowing right and doing right.

2. WISDOM

    - Ability to pursue a course of action in the face of adversity.
    - Courage without good judgment is futile and potentially harmful.
    - Intelligence is no substitute for Godly discernment and wisdom.
    - Learn from leaders who are always willing to learn.

3. PRIORITIES

    - A sense of priority in a sea of problems and possibilities.
    - The ability to decipher instantly the difference between urgent and important.
    - Pushing back the traffic to attend to the main task at hand.

4. ENERGY

    - Health equation: healthy spirit plus healthy body helps us maintain a healthy soul.

- An understanding of the necessity to sow energy to reap energy.
- Setting a pace that gives each 24 hour period maximum opportunity.
- The enemy loves to rob our energy!
- If the devil knows you live by your feelings, he will feed you everything you feel like.

5. PERSONALITY

- Confidence, strength, openness, courage, warmth, friendliness, security.
- The ability to smile and laugh and to make others smile and laugh.
- A leaders who can laugh helps warm peoples hearts, puts them at ease and helps to distract them from the painful realities and harshness that life can sometimes bring.

6. LOYALTY

- Great leaders are loyal people. When we are loyal we bind ourselves to a person, not just a project.

7. GENEROSITY

- Great leaders are generous with:
    - their embrace
    - their words
    - their hospitality
    - their time, their talent, their treasure
    - their lives

57

Mentoring and Discipleship

MENTOR:
A wise and trusted counselor, teacher, adviser, guide.

MENTORING:

- The word Mentoring comes from the Greek word meaning steadfast and enduring.
- It is usually defined as a sustained relationship between a youth and an adult. Or between peer ages at different stages of life.
- Through continued involvement, the mentor offers support, guidance, and assistance as the mentored person goes through a difficult period, faces new challenges or works to correct a problem.
- In particular, where parents are either unavailable or unable to provide responsible guidance for their children, mentors can play a critical role.

TYPES OF MENTORING:
The two types of mentoring are natural mentoring and planned mentoring.

- Natural mentoring occurs through relationship.
- Planned mentoring occurs through structured programs.

PURPOSE OF MENTORING:

1. Educational or academic mentoring
2. Career mentoring
3. Personal Development mentoring.

> "My chief want in life is someone who shall make me do what I can." - Ralph Waldo Emerson

DISCIPLESHIP:

"I am the Good Shepherd. The Good Shepherd risks and lays down His [own] life for the sheep. But the hired servant (he who merely serves for wages) who is neither the shepherd nor the owner of the sheep, when he sees the wolf coming, deserts the flock and runs away. And the wolf chases and snatches them and scatters [the flock]. Now the hireling flees because he merely serves for wages and is not himself concerned about the sheep [cares nothing for them]. I am the Good Shepherd; and I know and recognize My own, and My own know and recognize Me--Even as [truly as] the Father knows Me and I also know the Father--and I am giving My [very own] life and laying it down on behalf of the sheep. And I have other sheep [beside these] that are not of this fold. I must bring and impel those also; and they will listen to My voice and heed My call, and so there will be [they will become] one flock under one Shepherd. For this [reason] the Father loves Me, because I lay down My [own] life--to take it back again. No one takes it away from Me. On the contrary, I lay it down voluntarily. [I put it from Myself.] I am authorized and have power to lay it down (to resign it) and I am authorized and have power to take it back again. These are the instructions (orders) which I have received [as My charge] from My Father. Then a fresh division of opinion arose among the Jews because of His saying these things."
[John 10:11-19 AMP]

THE END!

58

Ministry Defined

10 THINGS MINISTRY LOOKS LIKE:

1. **Willing, able and available to serve.**
2. **Knowing that when the why is high, the cost is low.**
3. **Being part of the solution.**
4. **Knowing that my contribution matters.**
5. **Consistent and planted.**
6. **Heart first. Next capacity. Then gift.**
7. **Being on time.**
8. **Humility.**
9. **Whatever it takes.**
10. **Leading with my life.**

> "Instead, whoever wants to become great among you must be your servant - just as the Son of Man did not come to be served, but to serve, and to give his life as a ransom for many."
> [Matthew 20:26-28 NIV]

59

Mr. Right & Ms. Right

10 CHARACTERISTICS TO LOOK FOR:

1. Values
   (same book, same page, same sentence)

2. Kingdom first
   (Matthew 6:33)

3. Integrity
   (knows right, and does right)

4. Teachable
   (pride doesn't get in the way)

5. Responsible
   (never shirking)

6. Attitude
   (doesn't run when the going gets tough)

7. Committed to growing
   (spiritually and emotionally)

8. Knows who they are
   (identity is secure)

9. Chemistry
   (Songs of Solomon 1:2-5)

10. Finances
    (hard-working, good steward, faithful tither and sower)

My Ordinary Life

> "Good leadership involves responsibility to the welfare of the group, which means that some people will get angry at your actions and decisions. It is inevitable - if you're honorable." - Colin Powell.

When we realize that leadership is always the problem and always the solution (as reminded time and time again by Pastor Brian Houston), we will realize how important it is to keep track of our own life and take responsibility for its impact on others.

As a leader, my every day life is incredibly important.

> "Place Your Life Before God
> So here's what I want you to do, God helping you: Take your everyday, ordinary life—your sleeping, eating, going-to-work, and walking-around life—and place it before God as an offering. Embracing what God does for you is the best thing you can do for him. Don't become so well-adjusted to your culture that you fit into it without even thinking. Instead, fix your attention on God. You'll be changed from the inside out. Readily recognize what he wants from you, and quickly respond to it. Unlike the culture around you, always dragging you down to its level of immaturity, God brings the best out of you, develops well-formed maturity in you."
> [Romans 12:1-2 The Message]

5 KEYS TO MAXIMIZING MY ORDINARY LIFE:

1. My ordinary life

   The everyday routine of my life matters. Routine is awesome if it is on purpose but routine is dreadful if it is a bad habit. A great routine is to read our Bible every day, to pray every day, to exercise regularly. We need to remember that the Holy Spirit is with you every day. Our attitude matters every day. Our ordinary life affects our life and our leadership.

2. My sleeping

   As a leader, it matters who you live with. If it is within your power to choose flat-mates, then choose wisely. We obviously need to be very wise when it comes to whom we marry, because we will sleep in the same bed with whomever we marry for the remainder of your married life. Dating matters! Who you spend your most intimate time with matters. Who we are intimate with affects our life and our leadership.

3. My eating

   Many relationships are built across a dining table. Who we eat with matters. What we eat and drink matters. Being a good example matters. When we eat out, we need to live within our means. Is Starbucks in your budget? To give up a $3.50 coffee every day means a saving of $1,274 every year. Who we dine and recline with affects our life and our leadership.

4. My work

Having a great work ethic is vital to next level leadership. You may have the career of your dreams or you may be doing a job that you don't really enjoy. Whatever you do, work hard and be a blessing! And when you choose your job, whether it is the career of your dreams or a job to make ends meet, remember that where you work, when you work, how you work matters, and will affect your life and your leadership.

5. My walking around

Who we spend time with, where we spend time, why we spend that time all matters. Our friendships, our Facebook, our Twitter, our associations – all matter. Perhaps you feel as though there is a 'glass ceiling' on your leadership. This could be a simple matter of 'guilty by association'. As a leader it is always wise to assess who we spend time with and how fruitful our relationships are. Who we 'walk' with affects our life and our leadership.

"And do not be conformed to this world, but be transformed by the renewing of your mind, that you may prove what is that good and acceptable and perfect will of God."
[Romans 12:2 NKJV]

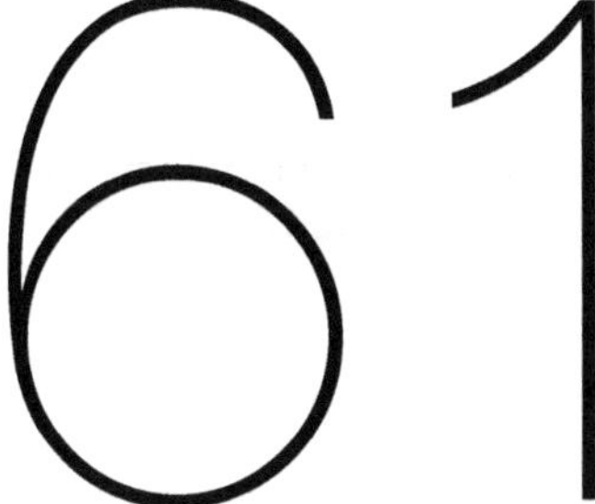

Next Level Leadership

1. **CHARACTER**
   Knowing right; doing right.

2. **COMMITMENT**
   A pledge, promise, agreement, obligation.

3. **CONSISTENCY**
   Steadfast adherence, 'stickability', loyalty, faithfulness, coherent solidity.

4. **CONVERSATION**
   Helpful informal interchange of thoughts or information, by words.

5. **CONNECTION**
   Anything that connects; the ability to be all things to all people in order to win some.

6. **COMPASSION**
   A feeling of deep sympathy and sorrow for another who is stricken by misfortune, accompanied by a strong desire to alleviate the suffering.

7. **CREATIVITY**
   The state of being that brings into existence that which does not yet exist.

8. CONTEMPLATE

   Something that is planned, fashioned, formed, devised, strategized, planned; intentional, calculated, estimated; an undertaking requiring concerted effort.

9. COUNT

   To consider; to take into account. A wise builder counts the cost before beginning his/her building project.

10. CALENDAR

    Any of various systems of reckoning time, and assisting in keeping to time.

11. COLLABORATION

    To work together, especially in a joint intellectual, emotional, physical and spiritual effort; to co-operate, assist, get together, join forces.

12. CARE

    Serious attention and devotion with action.

62

Pick Me! Choose Me!

> "Lift not up your [aggressive] horn on high, speak not with a stiff neck and insolent arrogance. For not from the east nor from the west nor from the south come promotion and lifting up. But God is the Judge! He puts down one and lifts up another."
>
> [Psalm 75:5-7 AMP]

We know that promotion comes from God but we also know that God uses people to promote people. It's up to us to be prepared so that we can be promoted. We need to do all that we can to learn, to grow and to not waste any seasons while we are awaiting our next promotion.

Perhaps you are considering signing up for a ministry internship. As Jodi Glickman wrote in her Harvard Business Review Blog on July 20, 2011,

> "Interns take note: energy and enthusiasm are no longer enough. You've got to bring something more meaningful to the table... "Interns, you might just have to come up with your own projects, figure out how to insert yourself into team projects, or just navigate this crazy world of work all on your own..."

Following are ways to help you prepare for promotion:

1. Take Responsibility

One of the best ways to be selected for promotion is help make your leader's life easier or better by thinking of where you can add value to the vision.

2. **Play to Your Strengths**

Work on your strengths and minimize your weaknesses. Recognize what comes easily and what is a struggle and sow your time accordingly.

3. **Use The Multiple-Choice Strategy**

Offering to help is good but offering tangible solutions is better. Always think of a few different options that could work and be prepared to follow through to completion whichever option is selected.

"The diligent find freedom in their work, the lazy are oppressed by work."
[Proverbs 12:24 The Message]

Poolside Reflections

It was a warm sunny afternoon just before the beginning of the school year as we gathered together to talk about life, the universe and of course, my favorite subject: Eternity.

1. Be in AND of the Word

"And so, dear brothers and sisters, I plead with you to give your bodies to God because of all he has done for you. Let them be a living and holy sacrifice—the kind he will find acceptable. This is truly the way to worship him. Don't copy the behavior and customs of this world, but let God transform you into a new person by changing the way you think. Then you will learn to know God's will for you, which is good and pleasing and perfect."
[Romans 12:1-2 NLT]

2. Church, Church, Church!

"All this energy issues from Christ: God raised him from death and set him on a throne in deep heaven, in charge of running the universe, everything from galaxies to governments, no name and no power exempt from his rule. And not just for the time being, but forever. He is in charge of it all, has the final word on everything. At the center of all this, Christ rules the church. The church, you see, is not peripheral to the world; the world is peripheral to the church. The church is Christ's body, in which he speaks and acts, by which he fills everything with his presence."
[Ephesians 1:20-23 The Message]

3. Follow the Leader

"Appreciate your pastoral leaders who gave you the Word of God. Take a good look at the way they live, and let their faithfulness instruct you, as well as their truthfulness. There should be a consistency that runs through us all. For Jesus doesn't change—yesterday, today, tomorrow, he's always totally himself."
[Hebrews 13:7 The Message]

4. Save the Dates

"He [Jesus] taught in their meeting places, reported kingdom news, and healed their diseased bodies, healed their bruised and hurt lives. When he looked out over the crowds, his heart broke. So confused and aimless they were, like sheep with no shepherd. "What a huge harvest!" he said to his disciples. "How few workers! On your knees and pray for harvest hands!"
[Matthew 9:35-38 The Message]

5. Conflict Resolution

"If your brother wrongs you, go and show him his fault, between you and him privately. If he listens to you, you have won back your brother. But if he does not listen, take along with you one or two others, so that every word may be confirmed and upheld by the testimony of two or three witnesses. If he pays no attention to them [refusing to listen and obey], tell it to the church; and if he refuses to listen even to the church, let him be to you as a pagan and a tax collector. Truly I tell you, whatever you forbid and declare to be improper and unlawful on earth must be what is already forbidden in heaven, and whatever you permit and declare proper and lawful on earth must be what is already permitted in heaven. Again I tell you, if two of you on earth agree (harmonize together, make a symphony together) about whatever [anything and everything] they may ask, it will

come to pass and be done for them by My Father in heaven. For wherever two or three are gathered (drawn together as My followers) in (into) My name, there I AM in the midst of them." [Matthew 18:15-20 Amplified Bible]

"There is but one Church in which men find salvation, just as outside the ark of Noah it was not possible for anyone to be saved."
– Thomas Aquinas

64

Poverty Mentality

1. **Mark 14**

   The people were indignant because Mary poured out the expensive perfume on Jesus.

2. **Matthew 25:25**

   The parable of the talents. The one who buried the talent saw his master as a harsh man (poverty perspective). Result: wicked and lazy.

3. **Mark 6:36**

   Jesus feeds 5,000. Disciples try to avoid the problem.

4. **Matthew 19:22**

   Rich young ruler. He had all the money he needed, but couldn't fathom himself without it.

5. **John 11: 21**

   Death of Lazarus. Martha thought Jesus was too late. Instead, Jesus performed a miracle.

6. **1 Samuel 15: 9**

   Saul and his army spared king Agag and the best of his sheep and cattle, thinking they were doing God a favor.

7. **1 Samuel 8:6**

   Israel begs for a king, because they wanted to be like everyone else.

8. **Matthew 26:15**

   Judas betrays Jesus, the Savior of the world, for a measly sum of money.

9. Job 2:9

   Job's wife loses all hope. She gives up in the midst of a storm.

10. Luke 14

   Jesus heals on the Sabbath. He gave everything, and lacked nothing.

"Poverty is the worst form of violence."
- Ghandi

10 Pressure Points

1. Relationships
   [healthy or unhealthy]

> "A good tree produces good fruit, and a bad tree produces bad fruit. A good tree can't produce bad fruit, and a bad tree can't produce good fruit."
> [Matthew 7:17-18 NLT]

Both healthy and unhealthy relationships add pressure to our lives. It is up to us to allocate appropriate time and energy to building healthy relationships and minimize how much time and energy we allow to be zapped from us because of unhealthy relationships. Perhaps that 'awkward' conversation is the very thing that will help bring health to what is currently unhealthy in a relationship you may be experiencing.

As leaders, we can't afford to waste our time and energy on relationships that don't bear good fruit. We should love all people, but we should invest primarily in people who are willing to help themselves.

2. Timing
   [finishing or hoarding]

> "All athletes are disciplined in their training. They do it to win a prize that will fade away, but we do it for an eternal prize."
> [1 Corinthians 9:25 NLT]

Finishing a project on time can add great pressure to our lives but so can 'holding the baby' adds even more pressure. Perhaps a project has been entrusted to you and you are not sure what to do with it and so you may be someone who tends to 'hold the baby' hoping it will all work out. The pressure this adds to your life and the pressure it adds to the team by inactivity and incompletion is usually greater than we realize.

Wisdom counts the cost before taking 'the baby' in the first place, so be sure you aren't a leader that hoards work so that when the deadline arrives, you have allowed the team around you to help bring the project to completion on time.

3. Punctuality
[early or late]

> "Servants (slaves), be obedient to those who are your physical masters, having respect for them and eager concern to please them, in singleness of motive and with all your heart, as [service] to Christ [Himself]--Not in the way of eye-service [as if they were watching you] and only to please men, but as servants (slaves) of Christ, doing the will of God heartily and with your whole soul."
>
> [Ephesians 6:5-6 AMP]

Our team knows that punctually is a value of our leadership. When we value time, we value people. This is something we need to address within ourselves regularly. It is easy to run a little behind and create a new habit of being late without even realizing the impact it has on us and on others. As a leader, it is always best to be 10 minutes early rather than 5 minutes late!

4. Planning
   [knowing or presuming]

> "And if you do not carry your own cross and follow me, you cannot be my disciple. But don't begin until you count the cost. For who would begin construction of a building without first calculating the cost to see if there is enough money to finish it? Otherwise, you might complete only the foundation before running out of money, and then everyone would laugh at you."
> [Luke 14:27-29 NLT]

Presumption is a pretty scary way to live your life. Imagine if the pilot of the plane you are about to board simply presumed that the aircraft had enough fuel to get to your destination, or that the engines were working properly. Pilots can't afford to presume anything. They need to check and re-check everything because people's lives are at risk. They have to know.

Leading people is a privilege and we should spend whatever time and energy necessary to actually know what we are doing, rather than living in the realm of presumption.

You can't know an outcome if you merely presume a process:

- Presume the process;
  presume the outcome.

- Know the process;
  Know the outcome.

5. Decisions
[wisdom or assumption]

> "Get wisdom; develop good judgment. Don't forget my words or turn away from them. Don't turn your back on wisdom, for she will protect you. Love her, and she will guard you. Getting wisdom is the wisest thing you can do! And whatever else you do, develop good judgment."
> [Proverbs 4:5-7 NLT]

If the Bible says we should 'get wisdom' then we should go ahead and get it! And where do we find wisdom? In the Word of God. One of the greatest challenges of leadership is trying to interact with people [specifically Christians] who don't read the Word of God and who assume that their opinion is correct simply because they believe so.

The Word of God gives us insight into wisdom and understanding more than any human instruction could ever offer us. Forming a Biblical opinion is healthy and necessary for quality leadership. It can add pressure to our lives because we learn not to settle for public popularity. My prayer is that you will learn as a leader to make decisions based on the Word of God and not just on the opinion of others.

6. Control
[of self or of others/situation]

> "But the Holy Spirit produces this kind of fruit in our lives: love, joy, peace, patience, kindness, goodness, faithfulness, gentleness, and self control. There is no law against these things!"
> [Galatians 5:22-23 NLT]

7. Resource
[wealth or poverty]

"Give, and you will receive. Your gift will return to you in full—pressed down, shaken together to make room for more, running over, and poured into your lap. The amount you give will determine the amount you get back."
[Luke 6:38 NLT]

8. Privilege
[inheritance or entitlement]

"LORD, you alone are my portion and my cup; you make my lot secure. The boundary lines have fallen for me in pleasant places; surely I have a delightful inheritance. I will praise the LORD, who counsels me; even at night my heart instructs me."
[Psalm 16:5-7 NIV]

9. Responsibility
[delegation or abdication]

"If the master returns and finds that the servant has done a good job, there will be a reward. I tell you the truth; the master will put that servant in charge of all he owns."
[Matthew 24:46-47 NLT]

10. Ministry
[passion or work]

"But whatever former things I had that might have been gains to me, I have come to consider as [one combined] loss for Christ's sake. Yes, furthermore, I count everything as loss compared to the possession of the priceless

privilege (the overwhelming preciousness, the surpassing worth, and supreme advantage) of knowing Christ Jesus my Lord and of progressively becoming more deeply and intimately acquainted with Him [of perceiving and recognizing and understanding Him more fully and clearly]. For His sake I have lost everything and consider it all to be mere rubbish (refuse, dregs), in order that I may win (gain) Christ (the Anointed One)."
[Philippians 3:7-8 AMP]

3 GREAT QUOTES:

1. "Hermits have no peer pressure."
   – Steven Wright

2. "No pressure, no diamonds."
   – Thomas Carlyle

3. "When the pressure comes, preferences give way while convictions hold firm."
   – Edwin Louis Cole

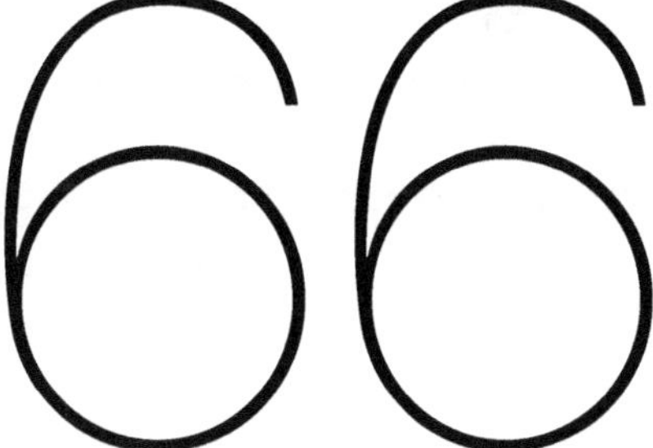

Privilege Problems

1. **Neglect**
   It is too easy to be come absorbed in the industry of ministry and to forget to look after yourself in body, soul and spirit. It is indeed a privilege to be a leader and the more you grow in influence the more crowded out life can become. Our goal is not to put ourselves first, of course, but to ensure that we have taken care of ourselves as a matter of priority. Keep working on becoming a better you and you will be a better gift to others.

2. **Entitlement**
   Inheritance is very different from entitlement. Inheritance is relational while entitlement is vocational. As leaders we need to remember that we aren't doing anyone a 'favor' when it comes to serving God and people, and we certainly shouldn't be focusing on the 'perks' of leadership. Entitlement can creep in when we lose sight of why we serve. Stay humble and watch what God will do!

3. **Offense**
   Offense doesn't just appear in our lives. There is a clear and gradual pathway that leads to an offended heart. It starts with a hurt and if that hurt isn't cleared up, it sets in as pain, and if the pain isn't cleared up, then a wall is established to somehow protect the pain. The pain remains and the wall is built. Offense is that wall. It is established by us on purpose because we weren't prepared to clear up the pain and hurt. Offense will take you out if you don't take it out.

4. Popularity

What the world that we are trying to reach doesn't need is celebrity leaders who believe their own press [good or bad]. We need leaders who understand the power of influence entrusted to them. We don't need branding and we don't need celebrating, we just need more JESUS to keep us real!

"Yes, everything else is worthless when compared with the infinite value of knowing Christ Jesus my Lord. For his sake I have discarded everything else, counting it all as garbage, so that I could gain Christ and become one with him. I no longer count on my own righteousness through obeying the law; rather, I become righteous through faith in Christ. For God's way of making us right with himself depends on faith. I want to know Christ and experience the mighty power that raised him from the dead. I want to suffer with him, sharing in his death, so that one way or another I will experience the resurrection from the dead! I don't mean to say that I have already achieved these things or that I have already reached perfection. But I press on to possess that perfection for which Christ Jesus first possessed me."

[Philippians 3:8-12 NLT]

Ready, Set, Go!

Below are the "Ready, Set, Go" Leadership Principles to help you win in life as a leader:

1. **READY**
   [are you ready?]

   - **Where have you positioned your 'set'?**
   - **When the 'race master' says, 'Take your marks!' where will you be?**
     - **Out of town?**
     - **Out to lunch?**
     - **Out of time?**
     - **Out of energy?**
     - **Out of sorts?**
     - **Out of touch?**
     - **Out of here?**
     - **Are you ready to take your mark?**
   - **When the Holy Spirit nudges you to 'get ready', do you procrastinate or do you take action?**

2. **SET**
   [are you set?]

   - **What values have you established?**
   - **What should be set in jelly?**
   - **What should be set in concrete?**
   - **Let's talk values... what are our values...?**
   - **What happens when our personal values transgress our corporate values, or vice-versa?**
   - **Do you have a consistent conflict of interest happening in your life?**

- If you do, you need to work it out, make decisions, go through the process and don't give up.
- When the 'race master' says, 'Get set!' what values are you setting?
- What example are you setting?
- What platform are you setting?
- What relationships are you setting?
- As leaders, we need to 'get set'.
- What I value determines the decisions I make.

3. GO

[are you going?]

- Are you moving forward?
- Are you running so fast you're out of breath because:
  - You're unfit?
  - You underestimated the distance?
  - You weren't really ready to run?
- Or maybe you didn't know where you were going and you have become lost along the way.
- When the 'race master' says, 'Go!' Do you know where you are going?
- Do you know why you are going?
- If you don't know where or why, you won't be able to last the distance.

"For everyone who calls on the name of the LORD will be saved." But how can they call on him to save them unless they believe in him? And how can they believe in him if they have never heard about him? And how can they hear about him unless someone tells them? And how will anyone GO and tell them without being sent?

That is why the Scriptures say, "How beautiful are the feet of messengers who bring good news!"
[Romans 10:13-15 NLT]

4. WIN
[are you winning?]

- Our purpose is to know Him and to make Him known.
- Our objective is to see the Kingdom established on earth.
- Our strategy is the local church.
- Our process is accountability.
- Our outcome is fruitfulness.
- There are many lost people who need us to WIN!
- IT'S TIME to win!

"Do you not know that in a race all the runners run, but only one gets the prize? Run in a such a way as to get the prize."
[1 Corinthians 9:24 NIV]

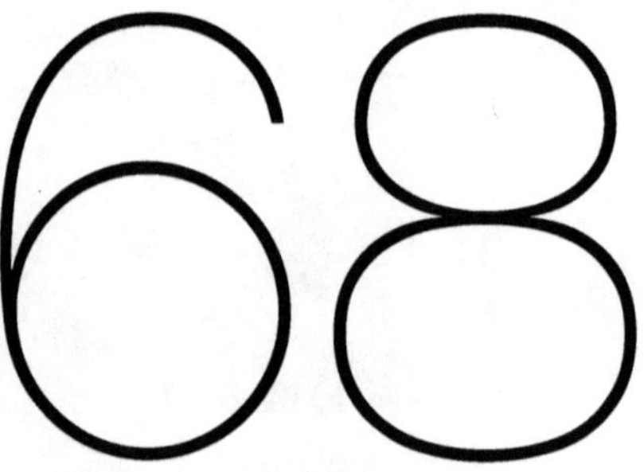

Reasons for Seasons

Before we can live the seasons well, we need to know how to read the seasons. And, we need to know the importance of maximizing our season, whatever the weather.

> "A right time for birth and another for death,
> A right time to plant and another to reap,
> A right time to kill and another to heal,
> A right time to destroy and another to construct,
> A right time to cry and another to laugh,
> A right time to lament and another to cheer,
> A right time to make love and another to abstain,
> A right time to embrace and another to part,
> A right time to search and another to count your losses,
> A right time to hold on and another to let go,
> A right time to rip out and another to mend,
> A right time to shut up and another to speak up,
> A right time to love and another to hate,
> A right time to wage war and another to make peace."
> [Ecclesiastes 3:1-8 Message Translation]

Whatever the season – whatever the weather, we need to remember what and who is constant.

- Summer or Winter
  [weather is constant and God is constant]

- Building or Dismantling
  [motion is constant and God is constant]

- War or Peace
  [fighting is constant and God is constant]

REASONS FOR SEASONS:

1. **Character development.**

2. **Once you have been through a season, it's easier to read the signs for the next time around.**

3. **Preparation.**

4. **Reaping what you sow – seeds don't change overnight.**

5. **Growth – spiritually.**

6. **Growth – financially.**

7. **Growth – capacity.**

8. **So we can be seasoned.**

9. **So we can be strengthened.**

10. **Our roots grow deeper, and we become planted.**

> **"Sow your seed in the morning, and at evening let not your hands be idle, for you do not know which will succeed, whether this or that, or whether both will do equally well."**
> **[Ecclesiastes 11:6 NIV]**

Reasons Why People Grow Familiar With Ministry

1. No Bible.

   First and foremost, they stop reading their Bible. And even if they are still reading their Bible, they forget that the Word is living, so they forget to ask Jesus to reveal to them new things.

2. No joy.

   The joy of the Lord is our strength. We must proclaim that over our lives. It works when you believe it!

3. No energy.

   They grow weary in doing good. They lose sight of the big picture, because they have positioned themselves ahead of Jesus and everyone else in their life.

4. No perspective.

   They have lost perspective, and somehow started to think that this life is all about them.

5. No clue.

   Their prayers turn towards their own wants, which is not bad per say, until it becomes one-dimensional. Scriptures turn into a tactic to get what they want. Matthew 6:33 becomes twisted. Instead of seek first His righteousness and all these things will be added to you, it becomes, "all things should be added to me because I am righteous.

6. No ability.
   They forget that this is an 'and' life. We can do 'this' and 'that'.

7. No patience.
   They lose patience of their dreams not coming to pass. They start to desire microwave outcomes. Proverbs 19:11 says, "A man's wisdom gives him patience; it is to his glory to overlook an offense."

8. No heart.
   They start to keep mental records of everything they do for Jesus. And when it doesn't get recognized by people, they start to harden their heart, forgetting that Jesus sees everything and lifts you up in due time.

9. No sacrifice.
   The day in day out life of anything tends to get familiar, but in Romans 12 the Bible tells us to take our everyday ordinary lives, our sleeping, eating, going to work, walking around life and place it before God as an offering. If we are not making a focused decision to do that daily, you will grow familiar.

10. No recognition.
    They don't recognize that what they are doing is ministry. They might be on the parking team, or serving coffee, and they see it as unimportant and small, rather than seeing it as part of the body. The smile they give someone might be the first smile that person has received in a long time.

Reasons to Give

"Give, and it will be given to you. A good measure, pressed down, shaken together and running over, will be poured into your lap. For with the measure you use, it will be measured to you."
[Luke 6:38 NIV]

1. The Bible says we should give.
2. Jesus gave and we follow His example.
3. It opens the door of people's hearts.
4. It enlarges our life.
5. Giving makes someone else's day.
6. We can.
7. Opens doors in our life.
8. God wants to bless us.
9. We will reap.
10. It builds our faith.
11. It's worth the investment.
12. It stores up treasure in Heaven.
13. I can expect a harvest.
14. It is a proven principle that works.
15. It causes favor with God and man.

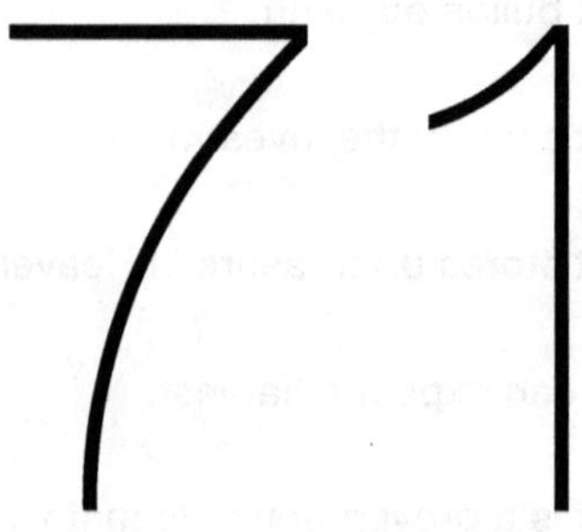

Runaway Bride

I had a funny dream about one of our team announcing that she was about to elope! The following are reasons people choose a 'runaway' wedding:

1. Spontaneous
   Couples love that, mostly because media portrays it.

2. Resource
   Vegas is cheaper than a ballroom.

3. Exclusion
   Good excuse not to invite certain people.

4. Freedom
   Simply because they can.

5. Fast
   Some couples just really want to have 'honest' sex.

6. Honeymoon
   Get away wedding, longer honeymoon...

7. Rebellion
   Proceed even if family and friends don't approve.

8. Easy
   Some people just don't want the big party planning

9. Do something different.
   Some people love the attention of uniqueness.

10. Running away from all things past.
    At least they think so.

72

Scissors, Paper, Rock

SCISSORS, PAPER, ROCK is a hand game played by two or more people. The game is often used as a selection method in a way similar to coin flipping, drawing straws, or throwing dice. However, unlike truly random selection methods, rock-paper-scissors can be played with a degree of skill. Especially if the game extends over many sessions with the same player(s), it is often possible to recognize and exploit the non-random behavior of an opponent.

- Scissors, represented by the index and middle fingers extended and separated.
- Paper, represented by an open hand, with the fingers connected (horizontal).
- Rock, represented by a clenched fist.

QUESTION: Are you ...
- SCISSORS?
- PAPER?
- ROCK?

1. SCISSORS
   [Cutting, divisive, dangerous.]

   "A gentle answer deflects anger, but harsh words make tempers flare. The tongue of the wise makes knowledge appealing, but the mouth of a fool belches out foolishness. The LORD is watching everywhere, keeping his eye on both the evil and the good."
   [Proverbs 15:1-3 NLT]

2. PAPER

[Light weight, blows around, fragile.]

"If any of you is deficient in wisdom, let him ask of the giving God [Who gives] to everyone liberally and ungrudgingly, without reproaching or faultfinding, and it will be given him. Only it must be in faith that he asks with no wavering (no hesitating, no doubting). For the one who wavers (hesitates, doubts) is like the billowing surge out at sea that is blown hither and thither and tossed by the wind. For truly, let not such a person imagine that he will receive anything [he asks for] from the Lord, [For being as he is] a man of two minds (hesitating, dubious, irresolute), [he is] unstable and unreliable and uncertain about everything [he thinks, feels, decides]."
[James 1:5-9 AMP]

3. ROCK

[Heavy weight, solid, immovable.]

"Who may worship in your sanctuary, LORD? Who may enter your presence on your holy hill? Those who lead blameless lives and do what is right, speaking the truth from sincere hearts. Those who refuse to gossip or harm their neighbor or speak evil of their friends. Those who despise flagrant sinners, and honor the faithful followers of the LORD, and keep their promises even when it hurts. Those who lend money without charging interest, and who cannot be bribed to lie about the innocent. Such people will stand firm forever."
[Psalm 15:1-5 NLT]

73

Servant or Apprentice

20 Differences Between Serving and Apprenticeship

1. A servant serves in general.
   An apprentice serves specifically.

2. A servant can be sporadic.
   An apprentice is consistent.

3. A servant lives on the first mile.
   An apprentice lives on the second mile.

4. A servant fulfills a task.
   An apprentice owns their project.

5. A servant serves a need.
   An apprentice creates solution.

6. A servant's service is optional.
   An apprentice is obligated.

7. A servant does what they can.
   An apprentice does whatever it takes.

9. A servant's role is geographical.
   An apprentice's role is anywhere at any time.

10. A servant waits for instruction.
    An apprentice takes responsibility.

11. A servant picks up for a moment.
An apprentice carries for the distance.

12. A servant stays for the final bow.
An apprentice stays till the curtains close.

13. A servant knows how.
An apprentice knows why.

14. A servant can get offended.
An apprentice defends others.

15. A servant notices a problem.
An apprentice fixes the problem.

16. A servant sees the task.
An apprentice sees the big picture.

17. A servant switches off.
An apprentice has one eye open.

18. A servant sets up.
An apprentice builds.

19. A servant dreams of a better life.
An apprentice builds a better life.

20. A servant reads the temperature.
An apprentice changes the atmosphere.

74

Signs That I Am Devoted

1. I am zealous

   "Zeal for your house consumes me, and the insults of those who insult You fall on me."
   [Psalm 69:9 NIV]

2. I am attached

   "Remain in me, and I will remain in you. No branch can bear fruit by itself; it must remain in the vine. Neither can you bear fruit unless you remain in me."
   [John 15:4 NIV]

3. I am loyal

   "So fear the Lord and serve him wholeheartedly. Put away forever the idols your ancestors worshiped when they lived beyond the Euphrates River and in Egypt. Serve the Lord alone. But if you refuse to serve the Lord, then choose today whom you will serve. Would you prefer the gods your ancestors served beyond the Euphrates? Or will it be the gods of the Amorites in whose land you now live? But as for me and my family, we will serve the Lord."
   [Joshua 24:14-15 NLT]

4. I am faithful

   "Let love and faithfulness never leave you; bind them around your neck, write them on the tablet of your heart."
   [Proverbs 3:3 NIV]

5. **I am consistent**

"The path of the righteous is like the first gleam of dawn, shining ever brighter till the full light of day."
[Proverbs 4:18 NIV]

6. **I am generous**

"For where your treasure is, there will your heart be also."
[Matthew 6:21 AMP]

7. **I devote myself**

"They devoted themselves to the apostles' teaching and to the fellowship, to the breaking of bread and to prayer."
[Acts 2:42 NIV]

75

Sleep On It

10 good reasons to sleep on it:

1. **To calm down.**
2. **To think yourself clear.**
3. **To seek wisdom.**
4. **To pray.**
5. **Play the movie out.**
6. **Daylight is brighter than night.**
7. **To gain peace.**
8. **To proceed with caution.**
9. **To help it go away.**
10. **Decide to act or not.**

"Do you see someone who speaks in haste? There is more hope for a fool than for them."
[Proverbs 29:20 NIV]

76

Sorry

10 reasons the words "I am sorry" are so powerful:

> Remember, for every minute you are angry, you lose 60 seconds of happiness!

1. It gives permission to start again.

2. Breaks down walls.

3. Releases weight and burden.

4. It says, "I care about our relationship."

5. It transitions the focus of self to others.

6. It lets go of regret and remorse.

7. It reminds you to move on and see big picture again.

8. It makes room for clear thinking

9. It reminds us we are human, which causes humility, which can lead us to God's perfection. And in him, we are made perfect.

10. The Bible says so.

77

Sowing and Reaping

- **We can't sow laziness and reap energy.**
  We have to sow energy to reap energy.

- **We can't sow strife and reap peace.**
  We have to sow peace to reap peace.

- **We can't sow good intentions and reap amazing outcomes.**
  We have to sow hard work and reap amazing outcomes.

- **We can't sow hope alone and reap financially.**
  We have to sow seed and faith to reap financially.

> "Sow for yourselves righteousness, [right standing with God] reap the fruit of unfailing love, and break up your unplowed ground; for it is time to seek the LORD, until he comes and showers righteousness on you."
> [Hosea 10:12 NIV]

> "Don't be misled: No one makes a fool of God. What a person plants, he will harvest. The person who plants selfishness, ignoring the needs of others—ignoring God!—harvests a crop of weeds. All he'll have to show for his life is weeds! But the one who plants in response to God, letting God's Spirit do the growth work in him, harvests a crop of real life, eternal life."
> [Galatians 6:7 The Message]

78

Steps to Starting Again

3 steps to starting again

1. Regret
2. Remorse
3. Repent

> "God Has Set Things Right
> But in our time something new has been added. What Moses and the prophets witnessed to all those years has happened. The God-setting-things-right that we read about has become Jesus-setting-things-right for us. And not only for us, but for everyone who believes in him. For there is no difference between us and them in this. Since we've compiled this long and sorry record as sinners (both us and them) and proved that we are utterly incapable of living the glorious lives God wills for us, God did it for us. Out of sheer generosity he put us in right standing with himself. A pure gift. He got us out of the mess we're in and restored us to where he always wanted us to be. And he did it by means of Jesus Christ."
> [Romans 3:22-24 The Message]

> "In a word, what I'm saying is, Grow up. You're kingdom subjects. Now live like it. Live out your God-created identity. Live generously and graciously toward others, the way God lives toward you."
> [Matthew 5:48 The Message]

79

Success

> "Intelligent people are always open to new ideas. In fact, they look for them."
> [Proverbs 18:15 NLT]

Are you motivated by success or are you motivated by failure? As leaders we can learn from both ends of the spectrum. I came across up a crazy book entitled, "How to be a complete and utter failure in life, work, and everything. 44.5 steps to lasting underachievement."

3 STEPS TO FAILURE:

1. Don't decide what you want.
2. If you do decide what you want, don't think about why you want it.
3. And if you do decide why you want it, commit to believing you can't have it.

Let's start at the beginning. The worst thing you can do, if you are truly committed to being one of life's failures, is to think clearly about what success means to you. We know that the best failures manage to avoid, at all costs, contemplating what success could actually look like.

On the other hand, it has been proven beyond any doubt, in study after study, that so-called high achievers have clearly defined what they want to do with their lives and have lots and lots of reasons why they want to do it. They have a crystal-clear vision of the future. They know what they love to do. And have set goals that will enable them to do what they love to do. Most importantly, these people also have a set of empowering beliefs that support them in creating the life they want to lead.

GOAL SETTING:

1. Make sure the goal you are working for is something you really want, not just something that sounds good.

2. A goal cannot contradict any of your other goals. For example, you can't buy a $10,000,000 house if your income goal is only $30,000 per year. This is called non-integrated thinking and will sabotage all of the hard work you put into your goals. Non-integrated thinking can also hamper your everyday thoughts as well. We should continually strive to eliminate contradictory ideas from our thinking.

3. Work on developing goals in every area of your life:
    - Marriage & family
    - Career
    - Leadership
    - Body & soul
    - Financial

4. Write your goal in the positive instead of the negative.

5. Write your goal out in complete detail. Instead of writing "a new home," write "a 4,000 square foot contemporary with 4 bedrooms and 3 baths and a view of the mountain on 2 acres of land."

6. Make sure your goal is high enough. Shoot for the moon. If you miss you'll still be in the stars.

7. This is the most important, write down your goals.

3 KEYS TO ACHIEVING YOUR GOAL:

1. Be very careful who you share your goals with, especially family and friends who are outside your 'dream zone'.

2. Review your goals regularly. Assess your progress.

3. Every time you make a decision during the day, ask yourself this question, 'Does it take me closer to, or further from my goal?' If the answer is 'closer to', then you've made the right decision. If the answer is 'further from', you've made the wrong decision. This could be in your attitude or action! Every decision, every day counts!

The difference between a goal and a dream is the written word. IT'S TIME to write it down!

> "If we don't change our direction, we are likely to end up where we are going." – Chinese Proverb

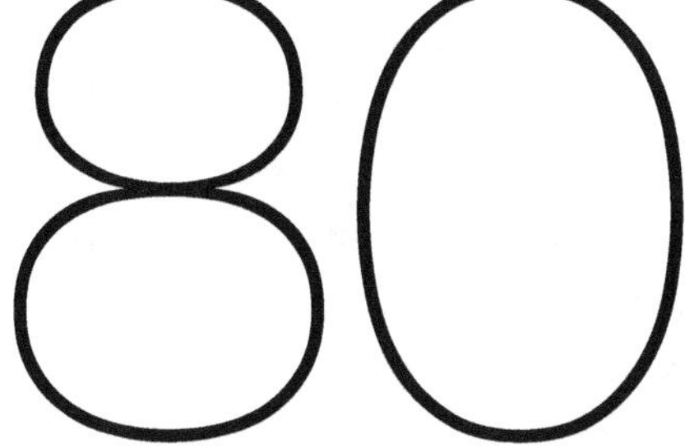

The Art of Delegation

Delegation is a skill of which we have all heard - but which few understand. It can be used either as an excuse for dumping tasks and responsibility onto the shoulders of followers, or as a dynamic tool for motivating and training leaders and followers to realize their full potential.

Delegation is primarily about entrusting your authority to others. This means that they can act and initiate independently; and that they assume responsibility (with you) for certain tasks. If something goes wrong, you remain responsible since you are the leader. The key is to delegate in such a way that things get done but that they can't go badly wrong.

The objective of delegation is to get the job done through other people. Not just the simple tasks of reading instructions and following them, but also some decision making and taking initiative. With delegation, your team is given the necessary authority to respond to situations entrusted to their care.

For example, if you ask for the trash to be taken out on Tuesdays and Fridays but the bins overflow on Wednesday, your empowered team will know to deal with the trash when it overflows, not just when you have specifically asked them to take care of it.

To enable someone else to do the job for you, you must ensure that the people following you:

- Know what you want.
- Have the authority to achieve it.
- Know how to do it.

One of the main fears about delegation is that by giving others authority, a leader loses control. This need not be the case.

If you train your team of followers to apply the same criteria as you would yourself (by example and full explanations) then they will be exercising your authority on your behalf.

To understand delegation, you really have to think about people. Delegation cannot be viewed as an abstract technique, it depends upon individuals and individual needs. The key is to delegate gradually. If you present someone with a task which is daunting, one with which he/she does not feel able to cope, then the task will not be done and your team of followers will be severely de-motivated. Instead you should build-up gradually; first a small task leading to a little development, then another small task which builds upon the first; when that is achieved, add another stage; and so on. This is the difference between asking people to scale a sheer wall and providing them with a staircase. Each task delegated should have enough complexity to stretch that member of staff - but only a little.

We need to help people win. Those following us need to feel confident. They need to believe that they will actually be able to achieve the task that has been given to them. This means that either they must have the sufficient knowledge, or they must know where to get it or where to get help. So, you must enable access to the necessary knowledge. If you hold that knowledge, make sure that those following you feel able to come to you; if someone else holds the knowledge, make sure that they are prepared for those following to come to them. Only if those following are sure that support is available will they feel confident enough to complete whatever task is required. You need to feel confident in those following: this means keeping an eye on them, but don't smother people. Lead by relationship and encouragement.

As leaders it is important for us to have a spirit of excellence that results in an expectation of high standards. When you delegate a job, it does not have to be done as well as you could do it, but only as well as necessary: never judge the outcome by what you expect you would do. When you delegate a task, realize that people are on a journey of learning and growth just like you and me!

We also must allow for failure. With appropriate monitoring, we should be able to catch mistakes before they are catastrophic; if not, then the failure is ours. As leaders, we need to focus on solution, and we need to help those following to be part of solving problems. When it comes to making mistakes, we need to be clear about our objectives. We need to make sure that those following us:

- Understand the problem.
- Feel confident enough to resume (and not give up).
- Implement effective procedures to prevent recurrence.

As Pastor Brian Houston always says, "Leadership is always the problem and leadership is always the solution." We need to take people on the amazing journey of discovery and help them see that problems are there for solving and we together can be part of the solution!

Perhaps you are wondering what you should delegate and what you shouldn't. As a wife I am not going to delegate my marriage to anyone else! As a Mum I am not going to delegate mothering or parenting, but I am happy to have a little help around the house with housework because we value 'Home Beautiful'. There is always the question of what to delegate and what to do yourself, and it is important to take a long term view on this: you want to delegate as much as possible to develop those following you to be as good as you are now.

A great starting point is to consider the activities you used to do before you were promoted in leadership. You used to do them when you were more junior, so someone junior can do them now. Tasks in which you have experience are the easiest for you to explain to others and so to train them to take over. You thus use your experience to ensure that the task is done well, rather than to actually perform the task yourself.

Whenever we have delegated anything, we still need to monitor the tasks we have delegated and to continue the development of our followers to help them achieve their goals. Remember, delegation without responsibility is abdication.

IT'S TIME for us to trust God and empower others!

> "Moses' father-in-law replied, 'What you are doing, this is not good. You and these people who come to you will only wear yourselves out. The work is too heavy for you; you cannot handle it alone. Listen now to me and I will give you advice, and may God be with you. You must be the people's representative before God and bring their disputes to him. Teach them the decrees and laws, and show them the way to live and the duties they are to perform. But select capable men from all the people- men who fear God, trustworthy men who hate dishonest gain- and appoint them as officials over thousands, hundreds, fifties and tens. "
>
> [Exodus 18:17-21 NLT]

81

The Big Event

10 HELPFUL QUESTIONS TO ASK BEFORE AN EVENT

1. What team am I on?

2. What is my call time each day/night?

3. What do I do if I am rostered onto two teams at the same time?

4. Should I wear my event shirt at the event? Why?

5. If I'm in the venue early can I save seats for me and my family and friends?

6. I'm rostered on to serve and I need to be there early, but I'm bringing some guests to the event. What do I do?

7. Do I need to bring food, or is there volunteer food provided?

8. Do we have a kids' program at the event?

9. As a volunteer, do I need to pay for the event?

10. My spouse wants to serve at the event – can they?

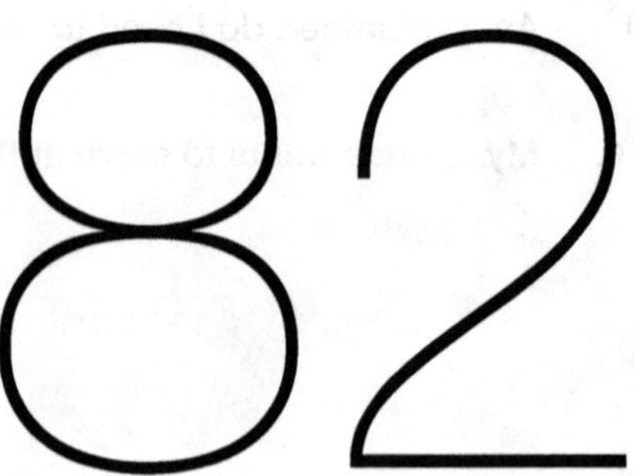

The Choice is Ours

Life is full of choices. Every moment of every day we are presented with countless opportunities to choose from. IT'S TIME to choose wisely!

1. Convenience or Conviction

"Do not be deceived and deluded and misled; God will not allow Himself to be sneered at (scorned, disdained, or mocked by mere pretensions or professions, or by His precepts being set aside.) [He inevitably deludes himself who attempts to delude God.] For whatever a man sows, that and that only is what he will reap. For he who sows to his own flesh (lower nature, sensuality) will from the flesh reap decay and ruin and destruction, but he who sows to the Spirit will from the Spirit reap eternal life."
[Galatians 6:7-8 AMP]

2. Selfish or Selfless

"I tell you the truth, unless a kernel of wheat is planted in the soil and dies, it remains alone. But its death will produce many new kernels—a plentiful harvest of new lives. Those who love their life in this world will lose it. Those who care nothing for their life in this world will keep it for eternity. Anyone who wants to be my disciple must follow me, because my servants must be where I am. And the Father will honor anyone who serves me."
[John 12:24-26 NLT]

SELFISH:
Devoted to or caring only for oneself; concerned primarily with one's own interests, benefits, welfare, etc., regardless of others.

SELFLESS:
Having little or no concern for oneself, esp. with regard to fame, position, money, etc.; unselfish.

3. Wounded or Warrior

> "These are the nations that GOD left there, using them to test the Israelites who had no experience in the Canaanite wars. He did it to train the descendants of Israel, the ones who had no battle experience, in the art of war. He left the five Philistine tyrants, all the Canaanites, the Sidonians, and the Hivites living on Mount Lebanon from Mount Baal Hermon to Hamath's Pass. They were there to test Israel and see whether they would obey GOD's commands that were given to their parents through Moses."
> [Judges 3:1-4 The Message]

4. Offended or Defender

> "Many Samaritans from the village believed in Jesus because the woman had said, "He told me everything I ever did!"
> [John 4:39 NLT]

Now let's go back to the beginning of that Bible story for some amazing insight into what happens when God reveals the truth in our lives ...

"Go and get your husband," Jesus told her. "I don't have a husband," the woman replied. Jesus said, "You're right! You don't have a husband—for you have had five husbands, and you aren't even married to the man you're living with now. You certainly spoke the truth!"
[John 4:16-18 NLT]

5. Believer or Unbeliever

"So don't worry about these things, saying, 'What will we eat? What will we drink? What will we wear?' These things dominate the thoughts of unbelievers, but your heavenly Father already knows all your needs. Seek the Kingdom of God above all else, and live righteously, and he will give you everything you need."
[Matthew 6:31-33 NLT]

6. Taker or Giver

"When you happen on someone who's in trouble or needs help among your people with whom you live in this land that GOD, your God, is giving you, don't look the other way pretending you don't see him. Don't keep a tight grip on your purse. No. Look at him, open your purse, lend whatever and as much as he needs. Don't count the cost. Don't listen to that selfish voice saying, "It's almost the seventh year, the year of All-Debts-Are-Canceled," and turn aside and leave your needy neighbor in the lurch, refusing to help him. He'll call GOD's attention to you and your blatant sin. Give freely and spontaneously. Don't have a stingy heart. The way you handle matters like this triggers GOD, your God's blessing in everything you do, all your work and ventures. There are always going to be poor and needy people among you.

So I command you: Always be generous, open purse and hands, give to your neighbors in trouble, your poor and hurting neighbors."
[Deuteronomy 15:9-11 The Message]

7. Market Place or Safe Place

"They arrived at Jerusalem. Immediately on entering the Temple Jesus started throwing out everyone who had set up shop there, buying and selling. He kicked over the tables of the bankers and the stalls of the pigeon merchants. He didn't let anyone even carry a basket through the Temple. And then he taught them, quoting this text: "My house was designated a house of prayer for the nations; you've turned it into a hangout for thieves."
[Mark 11:15-17 The Message]

8. Uniformity or Unity

How wonderful and pleasant it is when brothers live together in harmony! For harmony is as precious as the anointing oil that was poured over Aaron's head, that ran down his beard and onto the border of his robe. Harmony is as refreshing as the dew from Mount Hermon that falls on the mountains of Zion. And there the Lord has pronounced his blessing, even life everlasting.
[Psalm 133:1 NLT]

9. Interested or Committed

"When Jesus saw his ministry drawing huge crowds, he climbed a hillside. Those who were apprenticed to him, the committed, climbed with him. Arriving at a quiet place, he sat down and taught his climbing companions. This is what he said:

1. "You're blessed when you're at the end of your rope. With less of you there is more of God and his rule.

2. "You're blessed when you feel you've lost what is most dear to you. Only then can you be embraced by the One most dear to you.
3. "You're blessed when you're content with just who you are—no more, no less. That's the moment you find yourselves proud owners of everything that can't be bought.
4. "You're blessed when you've worked up a good appetite for God. He's food and drink in the best meal you'll ever eat.
5. "You're blessed when you care. At the moment of being 'care-full,' you find yourselves cared for.
6. "You're blessed when you get your inside world—your mind and heart—put right. Then you can see God in the outside world.
7. "You're blessed when you can show people how to cooperate instead of compete or fight. That's when you discover who you really are, and your place in God's family.
8. "You're blessed when your commitment to God provokes persecution. The persecution drives you even deeper into God's kingdom.
9. "Not only that—count yourselves blessed every time people put you down or throw you out or speak lies about you to discredit me. What it means is that the truth is too close for comfort and they are uncomfortable. You can be glad when that happens—give a cheer, even!—for though they don't like it, I do! And all heaven applauds. And know that you are in good company. My prophets and witnesses have always gotten into this kind of trouble. [Matthew 5:1-12 The Message]

10. Ideas Person or Implementer

"You should keep asking each other, 'What is the LORD's answer?' or 'What is the LORD saying?' But stop using this phrase, 'prophecy from the LORD.' For people are using it to give authority to their own ideas, turning upside down the words of our God, the living God, the LORD of Heaven's Armies."
[Jeremiah 23:35-36 NLT]

"The sluggard is wiser in his own eyes and conceit than seven men who can render a reason and answer discreetly."
[Proverbs 26:16 AMP]

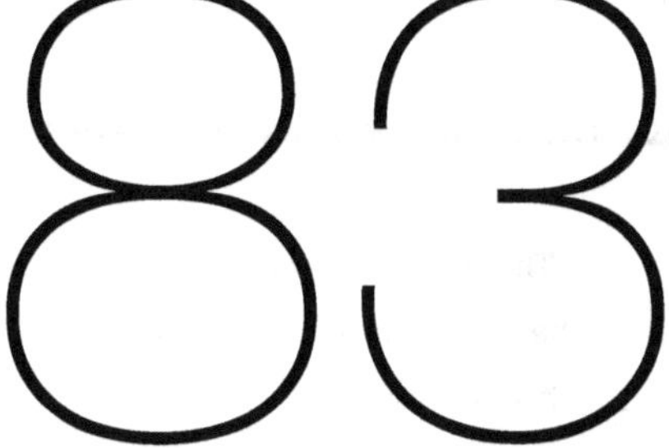
83

The Gospel Is

The Gospel of the Lord Jesus Christ is LOVE. The Gospel is described in many ways and we need to readily recognize and communicate what the Gospel is to others:

10 THINGS THAT THE GOSPEL IS:

1. The Gospel is the Good News of Jesus Christ.

2. The Gospel is the fact that He makes ALL things new.

3. The Gospel is Eternity in the hearts of men.

4. The Gospel is victory, once and for all.

5. The Gospel is spiritual food; bread of life.

6. The Gospel is the message written plainly for all to see and hear.

7. The Gospel is alive and well; active; never changing.

8. The Gospel is hope.

9 The Gospel is central; all else compares to it.

10. The Gospel is the truth; there's no getting around it.

> "There is no other message, just this one. Every creature under heaven gets this same message. I Paul, am a messenger of this message."
> [Colossians 1:23 The Message]

84

The Heart of a Leader

Our thinking as leaders always needs to go to the next level as we learn and grow and realize how much more we need to learn and grow. Our thinking affects our heart and our heart affects our thinking. Out of the abundance of our heart, our mouths and lives speak. What condition is your heart currently in? The condition of our heart determines the condition of our life.

> "One day Jesus told a story in the form of a parable to a large crowd that had gathered from many towns to hear him: "A farmer went out to plant his seed. As he scattered it across his field, some seed fell on a footpath, where it was stepped on, and the birds ate it. Other seed fell among rocks. It began to grow, but the plant soon wilted and died for lack of moisture. Other seed fell among thorns that grew up with it and choked out the tender plants. Still other seed fell on fertile soil. This seed grew and produced a crop that was a hundred times as much as had been planted!" When he had said this, he called out, "Anyone with ears to hear should listen and understand. His disciples asked him what this parable meant. He replied, "You are permitted to understand the secrets of the Kingdom of God. But I use parables to teach the others so that the Scriptures might be fulfilled: 'When they look, they won't really see. When they hear, they won't understand.' "This is the meaning of the parable: The seed is God's word. The seeds that fell on the footpath represent those who hear the message, only to have the devil come and take it away from their hearts and prevent them from believing and being saved.

> The seeds on the rocky soil represent those who hear the message and receive it with joy. But since they don't have deep roots, they believe for a while, then they fall away when they face temptation. The seeds that fell among the thorns represent those who hear the message, but all too quickly the message is crowded out by the cares and riches and pleasures of this life. And so they never grow into maturity. And the seeds that fell on the good soil represent honest, good-hearted people who hear God's word, cling to it, and patiently produce a huge harvest."
> [Luke 8:4-15 NLT]

The seed in this story is God's Word. Do you ever wonder why it is when God's Word is spoken, people receive it differently? This parable explains why. There is one of seed – God's Word, but there are four different grounds, which represent four heart conditions.

1. HARD HEART

> "Those along the traveled road are the people who have heard; then the devil comes and carries away the message out of their hearts, that they may not believe (acknowledge Me as their Savior and devote themselves to Me) and be saved [here and hereafter]."
> [Luke 8:12 AMP]

- This kind of heart has heard it all before.
- This kind of heart can't stand still long enough to believe.

- **This kind of heart is high maintenance, low yielding.**
- **This kind of heart will walk out, will walk away from God and from you.**
- **Statistically speaking, this kind of heart represents those we lose along the way, no matter how hard you try.**

2. SHALLOW HEART

"And those upon the rock [are the people] who, when they hear [the Word], receive and welcome it with joy; but these have no root. They believe for a while, and in time of trial and temptation fall away (withdraw and stand aloof)."
[Luke 8:13 AMP]

- **This kind of heart is led by feelings.**
- **This kind of heart is spiritually shallow.**
- **This kind of heart is hard work.**
- **This kind of heart draws attention to its withdrawn state.**
- **This kind of heart needs feeding, nurturing, stroking, encouraging...**
- **This kind of heart doesn't run away, it just sulks in the corner, waiting for you to come rescue!**

3. ANXIOUS HEART

"And as for what fell among the thorns, these are [the people] who hear, but as they go on their way they are choked and suffocated with the anxieties and cares and riches and pleasures of life, and their fruit does not ripen (come to maturity and perfection)."
[Luke 8:14 AMP]

- This heart isn't materialistic. This heart sees itself as 'realistic'. 'Realistically', it needs more money. 'Realistically', it needs more time for fun.

- In it's pursuit to alleviate life's real issues; this heart focuses on what it doesn't have, which causes more anxiety.

- God's Word says seek first the Kingdom then all these things will be added. This heart says seek first alleviating all of my issues.

- This heart wants what's right but goes about it the wrong ways.

- This heart is represented in the lives of many people, including leaders!

"Don't worry about anything; instead, pray about everything. Tell God what you need, and thank him for all he has done. Then you will experience God's peace, which exceeds anything we can understand. His peace will guard your hearts and minds as you live in Christ Jesus."
[Philippians 4:6-7 NLT]

4. HEALTHY HEART

"But as for that [seed] in the good soil, these are [the people] who, hearing the Word, hold it fast in a just (noble, virtuous) and worthy heart, and steadily bring forth fruit with patience." [Luke 8:15 AMP]

- This kind of heart is the heart of a LEADER.
- This kind of heart is stable.
- This kind of heart is steady.
- This kind of heart is believing.
- This kind of heart is trusting.
- This kind of heart is obeying.
- This kind of heart is fruitful.

85

The Role of a Leader

> **"Calling the crowd to join his disciples, he said, "Anyone who intends to come with me has to let me lead. You're not in the driver's seat; I am. Don't run from suffering; embrace it. Follow me and I'll show you how."**
> **[Mark 8:34 The Message]**

Copying actions isn't the same as "following the leader". There is a big difference between replication and reproduction. **For us to be effective leaders, marked with significance, we need to follow Biblical leadership patterns. We need to resemble Jesus!**

> "The next day Moses took his place to judge the people. People were standing before him all day long, from morning to night. When Moses' father-in-law saw all that he was doing for the people, he said, "What's going on here? Why are you doing all this, and all by yourself, letting everybody line up before you from morning to night?" Moses said to his father-in-law, "Because the people come to me with questions about God. When something comes up, they come to me. I judge between a man and his neighbor and teach them God's laws and instructions." Moses' father-in-law said, "This is no way to go about it. You'll burn out, and the people right along with you. This is way too much for you - you can't do this alone. Now listen to me. Let me tell you how to do this so that God will be in this with you. Be there for the people before God, but let the matters of concern be presented to God. Your job is to teach them the rules and instructions, to show them how to live, what to do. And then you need to keep a sharp eye out for competent men - men who fear

God, men of integrity, men who are incorruptible - and appoint them as leaders over groups organized by the thousand, by the hundred, by fifty, and by ten. They'll be responsible for the everyday work of judging among the people. They'll bring the hard cases to you, but in the routine cases they'll be the judges. They will share your load and that will make it easier for you. If you handle the work this way, you'll have the strength to carry out whatever God commands you, and the people in their settings will flourish also." Moses listened to the counsel of his father-in-law and did everything he said."
[Exodus 18:13-26 The Message]

THE ROLE OF A LEADER:

1. PRESENCE

Be there for people before God – being present matters. Leaders are present where they should be when they should be.
[Hospital bedside, birth of baby, significant milestones in kids lives.]

2. PRAYER

Let matters of concern be presented to God- don't try to be God.

3. TEACH

Teach people Kingdom rules and instructions – know what the 'Bible says".

4. EXAMPLE

Show them how to live and what to do. Refer to the parable of the talents in Matthew 25 and Luke 19, and remember: faithfulness is proven in the absence of the Master.

Leadership Development 5 Step Process:

1. I do, you watch, we talk
2. I do, you help, we talk
3. You do, I help, we talk
4. You do, I watch, we talk
5. Both find another person to do steps 1-4 with!

5. OBSERVE

Keep a sharp eye out for competent men [and women], who fear God, have integrity, are incorruptible. The word 'competent' means: appropriate, adequate but not exceptional. Leaders aren't born leaders, they become leaders!

6. APPOINT

Appoint them as leaders

B Believe in them
E Encourage them
S Support them
T Trust them

7. LEAD

Continue to judge hard cases while allowing routine cases to be handled by the appointed leaders making life easier for everyone.

"If you handle the work this way, you'll have the strength to carry out whatever God commands you, and the people in their settings will flourish also."
[Exodus 28:22 The Message]

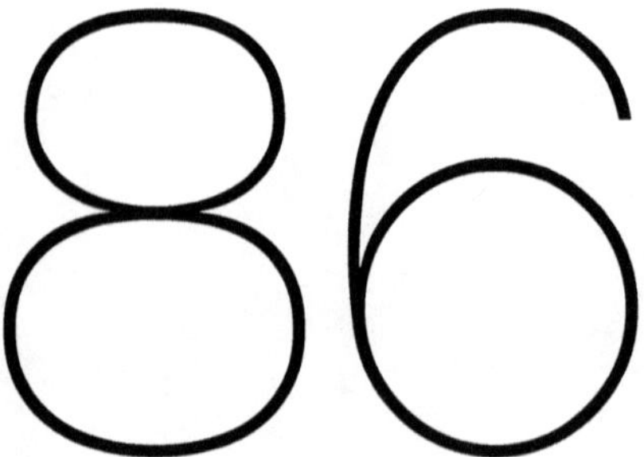
86

Things That Can Cause Our Leaders Grief

> "Be responsive to your pastoral leaders. Listen to their counsel. They are alert to the condition of your lives and work under the strict supervision of God. Contribute to the joy of their leadership, not its drudgery. Why would you want to make things harder for them?"
> [Hebrews 13:17 The Message]

1. Miscommunication that can cost relationship, money, time, etc.

2. Knowing right and doing wrong.

3. Own agenda.

4. Misrepresenting senior leaders or any other leaders.

5. Doing what's right in our own eyes when we've been told a different way.

6. Lack of accountability.

7. Not taking direction.

8. Not taking correction.

9. Being late.

10. Not saying anything when people are speaking negatively in your presence.

11. Starting a separate prayer meeting / sub culture.

12. Isolating yourself.

13. Resistance to what is happening.

14. Us vs them or men vs women.

15. Character / self-control.

16. Not respecting the time of senior leaders and other leaders.

17. Making big life decisions and telling your senior leaders after the face.

18. Mismanaging money.

19. Allowing hijacking to occur on your watch.

20. Not thinking yourself clear before you speak.

21. Planning a personal event that clashes with a church event.

22. Going away on vacation without delegating responsibilities properly.

23. Relational dysfunction.

24. Making excuses.

25. Not gathering people when our mandate is to gather.

To Conceal or Not to Conceal

10 THINGS A LEADER SHOULD CONCEAL:

1. Pastoral information that only belongs upward.
2. Answers to unnecessary questions.
3. Anything that would make someone stumble.
4. Personal finances – excess or lack.
5. If married, intimacy in relationship including sex life!
6. Anxiety.
7. Any past wrongs that would expose another person.
8. Disagreement of opinion.
9. Misunderstanding your leaders decision.
10. Stress.

"It is the glory of God to conceal a matter, to search out a matter is the glory of kings.
[Proverbs 25:22 NIV]

10 THINGS A LEADER SHOULD NOT CONCEAL:

1. Passion for Jesus.

2. Answers to questions...why behind the what.

3. Encouragement. [Hebrews 10:25]

4. Generosity.

5. Positive reports.

6. Your heart. A closed heart doesn't help anyone.

7. Blessing in your life, For His glory.

8. Your Testimony.

9. Your positive attitude.

10. Your Faith.

"Don't think you are going to conceal thoughts by concealing evidence that they ever existed."
- Dwight D. Eisenhower

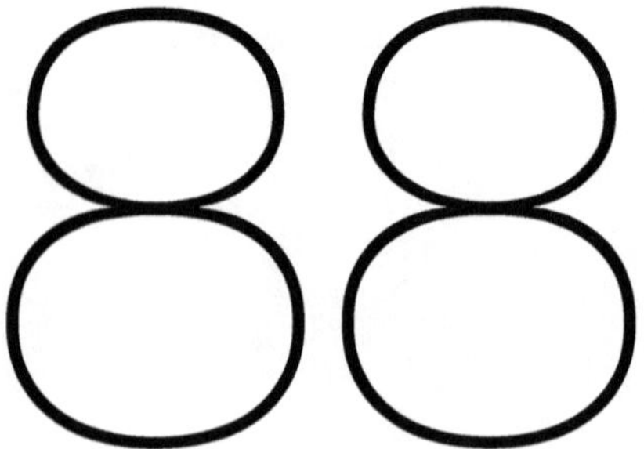

To Listen or Not to Listen

10 CHARACTERISTICS OF SOMEONE WE SHOULD LISTEN TO:

Everything listed below assumes that the person is a Christian, planted in a healthy church, and obedient to the call on their life. Otherwise, don't listen to them. Remember: confide in haste; regret at leisure.

1. Integrity
   Someone you should listen to is someone who practices what they preach. There's nothing worse than trying to follow the car in front of you when they put their blinker on right, but turn left.

2. Consistency
   You should listen to someone with it, for their life has been built by it.

3. Understanding
   When you're expressing how you feel about something, It's important that the listener tries to understand where you're coming from before they start to assume. To know is to love.

4. Authoritative
   People listened to Jesus partly because of the authority he had. I want to listen to someone who has God-given authority because it helps me understand where my place is.

5. **Seasoned**
   You should listen to someone who is seasoned. They have wisdom and you can learn from them.

6. **Loyal**
   You should listen to people who are loyal, because loyalty never abandons you.

7. **Encourager**
   You should listen to someone who encourages. As iron sharpens iron, so one man sharpens another.

8. **Generous**
   You should listen to someone who's generous, because you become like what you listen to. I want to be generous.

9. **Honest**
   You should listen to someone who is honest because they will tell you what you need to hear, even when you don't want to hear it. A wise person values honesty, and 'wants to hear what they don't want to hear'.

10. **Funny**
    You should listen to someone with a good sense of humor. They help bring joy into your life. It's good for your soul!

"Come and listen to my counsel. I'll share my heart with you and make you wise."
[Proverbs 1:23 NLT]

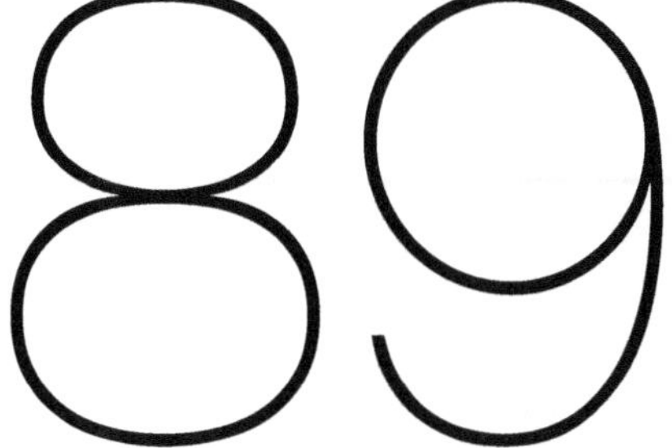

To Read or Not to Read

> "In all my perplexities and distresses, the Bible has never failed to give me light and strength."
> Abraham Lincoln

WHAT HAPPENS WHEN YOU READ YOUR BIBLE CONSISTENTLY:

1. Wisdom.
2. Revelation.
3. Faith.
4. Clarity.
5. Knowledge.
6. Relationship.
7. Truth.
8. Perspective.
9. Joy.
10. Peace.

> "It is impossible to enslave mentally or socially a Bible-reading people. The principles of the Bible are the groundwork of human freedom."
> Dr. Robert Milikan, Nobel Peace Prize winner

WHAT HAPPENS WHEN YOU DON'T READ YOUR BIBLE:

1. Offense.
2. Confusion.
3. Worry.
4. Insecurity.
5. Loss.
6. Isolation.
7. Religion.
8. Philosophy.
9. Fear.
10. Regret.

> "Ignorance of the Scriptures is ignorance of Christ."
> Sir Ambrose Flemming

Too Hard

10 THINGS WE THINK ARE TOO HARD:

1. Being single.
2. Exercise.
3. Finding time for kids.
4. Finding time for Bible reading.
5. Eating healthy.
6. Sharpening (character shaping).
7. Laying your life down.
8. Laundry/house work.
9. Commitment.
10. Follow through.

"We can throw stones, complain about them, stumble on them, climb over them, or build with them."
William Arthur Ward

10 THINGS THAT ARE ACTUALLY TOO HARD:

1. No purpose.

2. No destiny friends.

3. Doing life on your own.

4. Listening to parents fight.

5. Not being accountable to anyone.

6. Debt without being willing to tithe and sow.

7. A bad report with no faith.

8. Losing someone without understanding eternity.

9. Not having a home.

10. Trying to be someone you're not.

> "Faith is being sure of what you hope for and certain of what you do not see."
> [Hebrews 11:1 NIV]

Truth Time

I was on my way to an appointment stopped at a traffic light and picked up my phone to check something. As I reached down to grab it, a motorcycle cop drove right by my window. Needless to say I dropped my phone fast! This incident however started me thinking about what happened to my husband Jonathan just a few weeks earlier. He had been circling LAX airport waiting to pick up a guest arriving from Australia. The guest was caught up in customs and was delayed for quite some time, so Jonathan continued to check his phone until sirens started to sound! He was busted! As we all are every time we do something wrong. Even if no-one else sees us, God sees us.

When the police office pulled Jonathan over and asked him if he was texting, he had a choice to say yes or no... or did he? He did have a choice, but wisdom led him to say yes. If he decided to say no, then the police officer would simply take his phone and prove that he was texting.

We have raised our kids to understand that their worst truth is better than their best lie, and they are always going to benefit best from speaking the truth, even if it means they are going to get in trouble. It is all too easy to fall into a lifestyle of 'relative truth' rather than living in 'absolute truth'. The problem with living in 'relative truth' is that you will never know when 'absolute truth' will show up and prove what really happened. Here's some truth:

> "Jesus said to those Jews who had believed in Him, If you abide in My Word [hold fast to My teachings and live in accordance with them], you are truly My disciples. And you will know the Truth, and the Truth will set you free."
> [John 8:31-32 AMP]

If you were to print out your daily 'activity statement', how much activity would be 'negative activity'? Perhaps you can relate to one or more of these daily human behaviors:

- Done something you shouldn't
- Been somewhere you shouldn't.
- Looked somewhere you shouldn't.
- Thought something you shouldn't.
- Said something you shouldn't.
- Talked about something you shouldn't.
- Repeated something you shouldn't.
- Listened to something you shouldn't.
- Believed something you shouldn't.
- Reacted in a way you shouldn't.
- Spent time with someone you shouldn't.
- Spent money you know you shouldn't.
- Consumed what you know you shouldn't.
- Said yes when you know you shouldn't.
- Said no when you know you shouldn't.
- Lied when you know you shouldn't.
- Criticized when you know you shouldn't.
- Analyzed when you know you shouldn't.
- Laughed when you know you shouldn't.
- Replayed when you know you shouldn't.
- Stepped back when you know you shouldn't.
- Acted in a way you know you shouldn't
- Excused what you know you shouldn't.
- Co-signed when you know you shouldn't.
- Pursued something you shouldn't.
- Pursued someone you shouldn't.
- Forgot something you shouldn't.
- Yelled when you know you shouldn't.

> "Oh, the joys of those who do not follow the advice of the wicked, or stand around with sinners, or join in with mockers. But they delight in the law of the Lord, meditating on it day and night. They are like trees planted along the riverbank, bearing fruit each season. Their leaves never wither, and they prosper in all they do."
> [Psalm 1:1-3 NLT]

Let's be committed to living lives of integrity, where we know right and do right. Let's be committed to absolute truth as found in the person of Jesus Christ.

IT'S TIME!

> "Committing a great truth to memory is admirable; committing it to life is wisdom."
> William Arthur Ward

92

Wake Up! Get Up!

> "But make sure that you don't get so absorbed and exhausted in taking care of all your day-by-day obligations that you lose track of the time and doze off, oblivious to God. The night is about over, dawn is about to break. Be up and awake to what God is doing! God is putting the finishing touches on the salvation work he began when we first believed. We can't afford to waste a minute, must not squander these precious daylight hours in frivolity and indulgence, in sleeping around and dissipation, in bickering and grabbing everything in sight. Get out of bed and get dressed! Don't loiter and linger, waiting until the very last minute. Dress yourselves in Christ, and be up and about!"
>
> [Romans 13:11-14 The Message]

7 REASONS TO GET OUT OF BED IN THE MORNING:

1. It's a new day.
2. Things always look up in the morning.
3. It's a fresh start.
4. I have a purpose to fulfill.
5. I have one life to live and don't want to waste it.
6. People to see.
7. Places to go.

What God Wants

1. **God wants us to build His church**

   "Jesus came back, "God bless you, Simon, son of Jonah! You didn't get that answer out of books or from teachers. My Father in heaven, God himself, let you in on this secret of who I really am. And now I'm going to tell you who you are, really are. You are Peter, a rock. This is the rock on which I will put together my church, a church so expansive with energy that not even the gates of hell will be able to keep it out."
   [Matthew 16:1-18 The Message]

2. **God wants us to be in relationship.**

   "Love the Lord your God with all your heart and with all your soul and with all your mind and with all your strength."
   [Mark 12:30 NIV]

3. **God wants us to worship Him in spirit and truth.**

   "God is a Spirit (a spiritual Being) and those who worship Him must worship Him in spirit and in truth (reality)."
   [John 4:24 AMP]

4. **God wants to be acknowledged and remembered.**
   "Now it happened as He went to Jerusalem that He passed through the midst of Samaria and Galilee. Then as He entered a certain village, there met Him ten men who were lepers, who stood afar off. And they lifted up their voices and said, Jesus, Master, have mercy on us! So when He saw them, He said to them, Go, show yourselves to the priests. And so it was that as they went, they were cleansed.

And one of them, when he saw that he was healed, returned, and with a loud voice glorified God, and fell down on his face at His feet, giving Him thanks. And he was a Samaritan. So Jesus answered and said, Were there not ten cleansed? But where are the nine? Were there not any found who returned to give glory to God except this foreigner? And He said to him, Arise, go your way. Your faith has made you well."
Luke 17:11-19 NKJV]

5. God wants humanity to spend eternity with Him.

"For God so loved the world that He gave His only begotten Son, that whoever believes in Him should not perish but have everlasting life."
[John 3:16 NKJV]

6. God wants humanity to serve.

"Just as the Son of Man did not come to be served, but to serve, and to give his life as a ransom for many."
[Matthew 20:28 NIV]

7. God wants justice.

"I can't stand your religious meetings. I'm fed up with your conferences and conventions. I want nothing to do with your religion projects, your pretentious slogans and goals. I'm sick of your fund-raising schemes, your public relations and image making. I've had all I can take of your noisy ego-music. When was the last time you sang to me? Do you know what I want? I want justice—oceans of it. I want fairness—rivers of it. That's what I want. That's all I want.
[Amos 5:21 The Message]

8. God wants to provide for us.

"So don't be afraid, little flock. For it gives your Father great happiness to give you the Kingdom."
[Luke 12:32 NLT]

9. God wants fruit.

"He cuts off every branch of mine that doesn't produce fruit, and he prunes the branches that do bear fruit so they will produce even more."
[John 15:2 NLT]

10. God wants us to follow Jesus.

"But even as he [Peter] spoke, a bright cloud overshadowed them, and a voice from the cloud said, "This is my dearly loved Son, who brings me great joy. Listen to him."
[Matthew 17:5 NLT]

11. God wants us to love Him.

"Jesus replied: "'Love the Lord your God with all your heart and with all your soul and with all your mind.' This is the first and greatest commandment.
[Matthew 22:39]

12. God wants us to love others.

"And the second is like it: 'Love your neighbor as yourself.'"
[Matthew 22:37-38]

What is Understood

> "Wisdom is enshrined in an understanding heart; wisdom is not found among fools."
> [Proverbs 14:33 NLT]

What is understood need not be discussed. As leaders we need to seek to understand more than we desire to be understood. The more you live life as a leader the more you realize that not everyone will understand you, even when you go to great lengths to help them.

We need to be careful to listen before talking – we need to take the time to understand people. To know is to love.

The real key to your influence as a leader is your own personal example – your conduct. Your private performance must align with your public performance. Unless people trust you and believe you understand them, they will be too afraid or perhaps defensive to be influenced. Skills of empathic listening must be built on a character that inspires openness and trust and high emotional bank accounts.

When another person is speaking, we usually "listen" at one of four levels: ignoring, pretending, selective listening, or attentive listening. We should be using the fifth, highest form of listening - empathic listening. Empathic listening is listening with intent to understand the other person's frame of reference and feelings. You must listen with your ears, your eyes and your heart.

Empathic listening takes time, but not as much time as correcting misunderstandings, including living with problems and the results of not giving the people you care about 'clear air'.

Knowing how to be understood is as important as seeking to understand in reaching 'win/win' solutions, and requires courage.

The Greek philosophy of Ethos, Pathos, and Logos gives the sequence for effective communication. Ethos is your personal creditability. Pathos is the empathic side. Logos is the reasoning side. Most people go straight to the logical side without first establishing their character and building the relationship.

When we really deeply understand each other, we open the door to creative solutions.

IT'S TIME to understand!

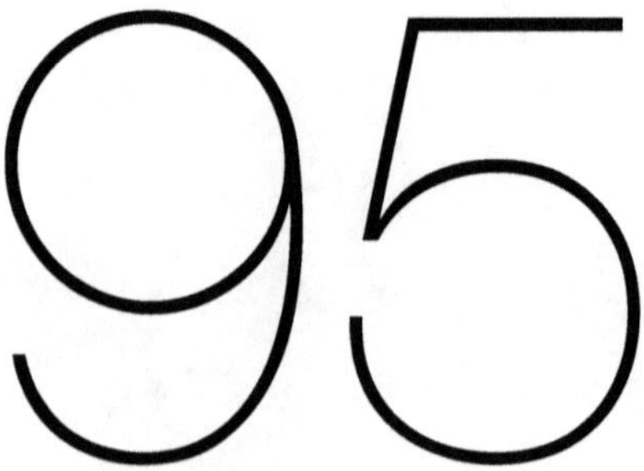

What Just Happened?

Leadership doesn't remove us from our humanity. We still have to deal with our 'stuff'. Jesus opened His mouth and taught His disciples. The disciples followed Jesus around watching Him closely. It was still essential for Him to take them aside and teach them. It was essential for Jesus to help them make sense of 'what just happened'.

> "When Jesus saw his ministry drawing huge crowds, he climbed a hillside. Those who were apprenticed to him, the committed, climbed with him. Arriving at a quiet place, he sat down and taught his climbing companions. This is what he said: "You're blessed when ..."
> [Matthew 5 The Message]

1. You're at the end of your rope.
2. You feel you've lost what's most dear to you.
3. You're content with just who you are.
4. You've worked up a good appetite for God.
5. You care.
6. You can get your inside world – your mind and heart – put right.
7. You can show people how to co-operate instead of compete or fight.
8. Your commitment to God provokes persecution.
9. People put you down or throw you out or speak lies about you to discredit God.

When 'life happens' we need to remember that we are blessed, even when we are wondering, 'what just happened?'

Jesus desires us to be His followers, in word and deed:

1. Follow His example.
2. Listen to His words.
3. Do His work.
4. Accept His will.
5. Fulfill His purpose.

The enemy wants us to sit down and shut up from the inside out so that we will become ineffective. If you are in a season where you are feeling confused, conflicted, compromised, maybe you are wondering, 'what just happened?'

10 OPTIONS WE HAVE IN EVERY SEASON:

1. Humility vs Pride
[servant leadership vs kingly leadership]

"Blessed (happy, to be envied, and spiritually prosperous--with life-joy and satisfaction in God's favor and salvation, regardless of their outward conditions) are the poor in spirit (the humble, who rate themselves insignificant), for theirs is the kingdom of heaven!"
[Matthew 5:3 AMP]

2. Loss vs Gain
[perspective]

"Blessed and enviably happy [with a happiness produced by the experience of God's favor and especially conditioned by the revelation of His matchless grace] are those who mourn, for they shall be comforted!"
[Matthew 5:4 AMP]

3. Finisher vs Quitter
[inner strength vs outward conditions]

"Blessed (happy, blithesome, joyous, spiritually prosperous--with life-joy and satisfaction in God's favor and salvation, regardless of their outward conditions) are the meek (the mild, patient, long-suffering), for they shall inherit the earth!"
[Matthew 5:5 AMP]

4. Fear of God vs Fear of Man
[dissatisfied vs satisfied]

"Blessed and fortunate and happy and spiritually prosperous (in that state in which the born-again child of God enjoys His favor and salvation) are those who hunger and thirst for righteousness (uprightness and right standing with God), for they shall be completely satisfied!"
[Matthew 5:6 AMP]

5. Merciful vs Material
[all about others vs all about me]

"Blessed (happy, to be envied, and spiritually prosperous--with life-joy and satisfaction in God's favor and salvation, regardless of their outward conditions) are the merciful, for they shall obtain mercy!"
[Matthew 5:7 AMP]

6. Grace vs Striving
[God's great work vs my good works]

"Blessed (happy, enviably fortunate, and spiritually prosperous--possessing the happiness produced by the experience of God's

favor and especially conditioned by the revelation of His grace, regardless of their outward conditions) are the pure in heart, for they shall see God!"
[Matthew 5:8 AMP]

7. Problem Solver vs Problem Maker
[leadership the solution vs leadership the problem]

"Blessed (enjoying enviable happiness, spiritually prosperous--with life-joy and satisfaction in God's favor and salvation, regardless of their outward conditions) are the makers and maintainers of peace, for they shall be called the sons of God!"
[Matthew 5:9 AMP]

8. Silent vs Self-Protective
[God justice vs our own justice]

"Blessed and happy and enviably fortunate and spiritually prosperous (in the state in which the born-again child of God enjoys and finds satisfaction in God's favor and salvation, regardless of his outward conditions) are those who are persecuted for righteousness' sake (for being and doing right), for theirs is the kingdom of heaven!"
[Matthew 5:10 AMP]

9. Persecuted vs Punished
[doing the right thing vs doing the wrong thing]

"Blessed (happy, to be envied, and spiritually prosperous--with life-joy and satisfaction in God's favor and salvation, regardless of your outward conditions) are you when people revile you and persecute you and say all kinds of evil things against you falsely on My account."
[Matthew 5:11 AMP]

10. In Good Company vs Isolated [wisdom relationships vs lone ranger]

"Be glad and supremely joyful, for your reward in heaven is great (strong and intense), for in this same way people persecuted the prophets who were before you."
[Matthew 5:12 AMP]

"When it is dark enough, you can see the stars."
Ralph Waldo Emerson

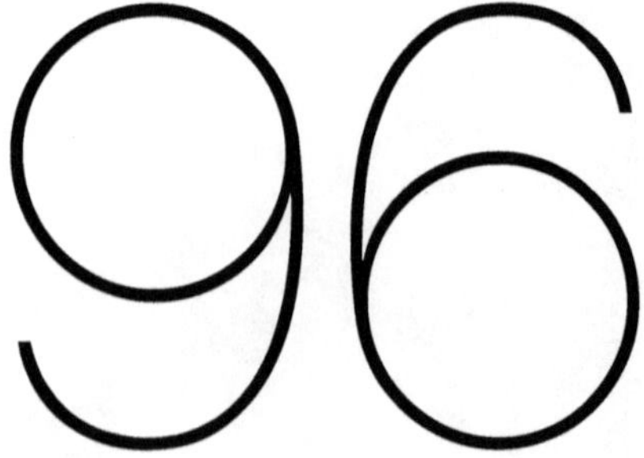

What Sentence Are You Serving?

"Everything you now do is something you have chosen to do. Some people don't want to believe that. But if you're over age twenty-one, your life is what you're making of it. To change your life, you need to change your priorities."
John C Maxwell

1. NEW LIFE or OLD LIFE

"Could it be any clearer? Our old way of life was nailed to the cross with Christ, a decisive end to that sin-miserable life—no longer at sin's every beck and call! What we believe is this: If we get included in Christ's sin-conquering death, we also get included in his life-saving resurrection. We know that when Jesus was raised from the dead it was a signal of the end of death-as-the-end. Never again will death have the last word. When Jesus died, he took sin down with him, but alive he brings God down to us. From now on, think of it this way: Sin speaks a dead language that means nothing to you; God speaks your mother tongue, and you hang on every word. You are dead to sin and alive to God. That's what Jesus did. That means you must not give sin a vote in the way you conduct your lives. Don't give it the time of day. Don't even run little errands that are connected with that old way of life. Throw yourselves wholeheartedly and full-time—remember, you've been raised from the dead!—into God's way of doing things. Sin can't tell you how to live. After all, you're not living under that old tyranny any longer. You're living in the freedom of God."

[Romans 6:11-14 The Message]

2. PLEASING GOD or PEOPLE PLEASING

"Even though I am free of the demands and expectations of everyone, I have voluntarily become a servant to any and all in order to reach a wide range of people: religious, nonreligious, meticulous moralists, loose-living immoralists, the defeated, the demoralized—whoever. I didn't take on their way of life. I kept my bearings in Christ—but I entered their world and tried to experience things from their point of view. I've become just about every sort of servant there is in my attempts to lead those I meet into a God-saved life. I did all this because of the Message. I didn't just want to talk about it; I wanted to be in on it!"
[1 Corinthians 9:19-23 The Message]

3. TAKING A STAND or WEARING A HARNESS

"Christ has set us free to live a free life. So take your stand! Never again let anyone put a harness of slavery on you."
[Galatians 5:1 The Message]

"How we spend our days is, of course, how we spend our lives."
Annie Dillard

What Husbands Really Want

CHICKTIME WIFE CONFESSIONS:

1. He wants to know that I'm happy and content.
2. He wants me to be fun!
3. He wants me to care about the way that I look and the way I carry myself.
4. He wants us to agree and be on the same page of where we are in life!
5. He wants me to be financially conscious.
6. I'm the person that he opens up to the most, so he wants me to be a good listener.
7. He wants me to challenge him when I believe he's wrong, even though that's hard for him to take.
8. He wants me to be a hard worker.
9. Sex of course!!! :) But more importantly he wants me to be open and honest about what I like/don't like, want/don't want.
10. He wants me to be patient with him when I don't understand where he's coming from.
11. He wants me to build healthy relationships with the people in my world.
12. He wants me to make time for him and plan exciting date nights!

13. He wants me to be passionate about Jesus.

14. He wants me to be passionate about church.

15. He wants me to have good friends.

16. He wants me to make sure he has clean undies!

17. He wants me to have food in the fridge.

19. He wants me to be able to entertain myself.

20. He wants me to be clear instead of hinting.

21. He wants me to tell him what's wrong when he knows there's something wrong.

22. He wants me to build the church with him – together!

23. He wants to provide for me.

24. He wants me to stop everything I'm doing to greet him with a kiss when he walks in the door.

25. He wants me to honor him.

26. He wants me to support him in his dreams.

27. He wants me to stop telling him how to drive [!]

28. He wants me to build him up not tear him down with my words.

29. He wants to rely on God's strength and not his own.

30. He wants me to be confident and secure.

31. He wants a delicious and healthy home-cooked meal whenever possible.

32. He wants to live in a clean, tidy and organized home.

33. He wants to know that I value his efforts.

34. He wants me to flourish and live a purposeful and fruitful life.

35. He wants me to be beautiful inside and out.

36. He wants me to make an effort with my appearance.

37. He wants me to support him 100%.

38. He wants his life with me to be a journey of adventure instead of day after day of boring predictability.

39. He wants me to be understanding and not to react to a moment of weakness.

40. He wants me not to nag in the midst of a stressful situation.

41. He wants me to help him prepare and produce what God has called us to do together.

42. He wants me to submit.

43. He wants me to be a hands on, interactive mother to our kids.

44. He wants me to be wise and to think clearly and plan ahead.

45. He wants me to be a good steward and not wasteful.

46. He wants me to be generous to others with my time, talent and treasure.

47. He wants intimacy.

48. He wants my complete trust in him.

49. He wants me to share in his passions.

50. He wants me to allow him to comfort me when I'm sad or frustrated.

51. He wants me to be forgiving and not to hold grudges.

52. He wants me to celebrate his wins with him.

53. He wants me to give him my undivided attention when he needs it.

54. He wants me to be honest with him and not manipulative.

55. He wants me to be playful with him.

56. He wants to hear words of encouragement.

57. He wants to read words of encouragement.

58. He wants me to let him watch TV in peace.

59. He wants me to stop telling him what to do.

60. He wants me to have a healthy body, soul and spirit.

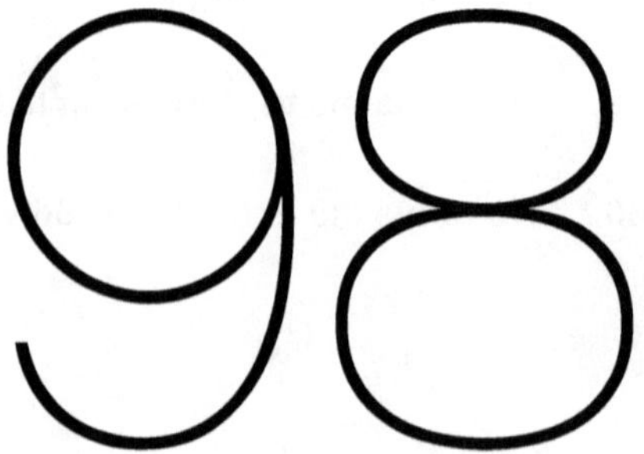

What's My Problem?

"We can rejoice, too, when we run into problems and trials, for we know that they help us develop endurance. And endurance develops strength of character, and character strengthens our confident hope of salvation."
[Romans 5:3-4 NLT]

1. PERSONAL PROBLEMS

"Turn to me and have mercy, for I am alone and in deep distress. My problems go from bad to worse. Oh, save me from them all!"
[Psalm 25:16-17 NLT]

2. LEADERSHIP PROBLEMS

"This man Daniel, whom the king named Belteshazzar, has exceptional ability and is filled with divine knowledge and understanding. He can interpret dreams, explain riddles, and solve difficult problems. Call for Daniel, and he will tell you what the writing means."
[Daniel 5:12 NLT]

3. GOD'S PROBLEM SOLVING

"God went for the jugular when he sent his own Son. He didn't deal with the problem as something remote and unimportant. In his Son, Jesus, he personally took on the human condition, entered the disordered mess of struggling humanity in order to set it right once and for all."
[Romans 8:3 The Message]

Why Gather?

MARTIN LUTHER :
"To gather with God's people in united adoration of the Father is as necessary to the Christian life as prayer."

JULIA A'BELL:
"Why should women gather? Women should gather strategically for friendship and strategically around a cause. Women should gather to understand the value placed upon them by God and they should gather to place value upon others who don't necessarily understand their value in God. They should gather because it's fun, and because there is nothing like getting together with 'the girls'. I believe women are rising up all across the earth. And God is using his girls to be his hands, feet & voice in both their local and global communities. God will use you... It's all a simple matter of making yourself available & saying 'yes' to his call."

CHRISTINE CAINE:
"Why are you so passionate about gathering the global Sisterhood? I am committed to empowering the global Sisterhood because I believe we cannot fulfill the great commission without gathering, equipping and mobilizing half of the body of Christ. Women are great influencers and have the capacity to do great works for the glory of Christ. Everything I do with and for women flows from the heartbeat of my Senior Pastor Bobbie Houston and the mandate of the Colour Sisterhood globally."

DIANNE WILSON
"Reach the lost. Equip the saints. Mobilize the army."
Keep reading...!

1. WHY GATHER?
To Take Sides

"He who is not with Me [definitely on My side] is against Me, and he who does not [definitely] gather with Me and for My side scatters."
[Matthew 12:30 AMP]

We need to be certain that there are two sides – Jesus on one side and the devil on the other. It's up to us to make a stand. We need to form an opinion that is Jesus' opinion. We need to get some traction, get some grunt and be prepared to fight for people's lives. We need to remember that we don't wrestle people, we wrestle spiritual principalities and powers! Let's stop fighting with people and start fighting the real enemy – the devil!

2. WHY GATHER?
To Take Knocks

"The Story of the Wedding Banquet
Jesus responded by telling still more stories. "God's kingdom," he said, "is like a king who threw a wedding banquet for his son. He sent out servants to call in all the invited guests. And they wouldn't come! [strike 1] "He sent out another round of servants, instructing them to tell the guests, 'Look, everything is on the table, the prime rib is ready for carving. Come to the feast!' They only shrugged their shoulders and went off, one to weed his garden, another to work in his shop. The rest, with nothing better to do, beat up on the messengers and then killed them. The king was outraged and sent his soldiers to destroy those thugs and level their city. [strike 2]. "Then he told his servants, 'We have a

> wedding banquet all prepared but no guests. The ones I invited weren't up to it. "Go out into the busiest intersections in town and invite anyone you find to the banquet.' The servants went out on the streets and rounded up everyone they laid eyes on, good and bad, regardless. And so the banquet was on—every place filled. [3 strikes and the hungry were in]."
> [Matthew 22:1-10 The Message]

When it comes to gathering people, many people don't persist past 'strike 1'. And to persist past 'strike 2' means we need to be willing to suffer persecution to reach people. We have to have the courage of our conviction to reach and gather people for Jesus! IT'S TIME!

3. WHY GATHER?
   To Take Root

> "Jesus speaking: "Yes, I am the vine; you are the branches. Those who remain in me, and I in them, will produce much fruit. For apart from me you can do nothing. Anyone who does not remain in me is thrown away like a useless branch and withers. Such branches are gathered into a pile to be burned. But if you remain in me and my words remain in you, you may ask for anything you want, and it will be granted! When you produce much fruit, you are my true disciples. This brings great glory to my Father."
> [John 15:5-8 NLT]

We need to help people who are wilting from disconnection. Our fruit is seen when people following us are fruitful. how many people in your life are fruitful? Connection brings fruit and isolation brings dysfunction.

4. WHY GATHER?
To Take Ground

"He [Jesus] pressed them [His disciples], "And how about you? Who do you say I am?" Simon Peter said, "You're the Christ, the Messiah, the Son of the living God." Jesus came back, "God bless you, Simon, son of Jonah! You didn't get that answer out of books or from teachers. My Father in heaven, God himself, let you in on this secret of who I really am. And now I'm going to tell you who you are, really are. You are Peter, a rock. This is the rock on which I will put together my church, a church so expansive with energy that not even the gates of hell will be able to keep it out. "And that's not all. You will have complete and free access to God's kingdom, keys to open any and every door: no more barriers between heaven and earth, earth and heaven. A yes on earth is yes in heaven. A no on earth is no in heaven."
[Matthew 16:18-25 NLT]

When we build His Church we push back darkness. When one soul is won into Heaven, one soul is taken from darkness. We are an army in formation to take ground away from the enemy. IT'S TIME!

5. WHY GATHER?
To Take Back

"The thief comes only in order to steal and kill and destroy. I came that they may have and enjoy life, and have it in abundance (to the full, till it overflows)."
[John 10:10 AMP]

In the eloquent words of Christine Caine, "The enemy is a PIG!" He has ripped off so many people we know. Just imagine those we don't know. This is our season to see people redeemed and restored. The enemy is a thief of peace. The enemy is a killer of dreams. The enemy is a destroyer of lives. Everyone needs a Savior. We all need a Savior!

LET'S DO THIS!

1. Take sides for Jesus.
2. Take knocks for Jesus.
3. Take root for Jesus.
4. Take ground for Jesus.
5. Take back for Jesus.

"Coming together is a beginning; keeping together is progress; working together is success."
Henry Ford

100

Words of a Leader

We need to be good with our words upwards, sideways, downwards.

1. Please.
    - It says may I have something you have?
    - If you don't use the please word, your leadership is under threat.
    - It helps express respect, a humble heart.

2. Thank you.
    - It says you have given me something I didn't have.
    - They are two of the most generous words you can give to someone.

3. Yes.
    - Let your yes be yes, rather than yep or yup!
    - It helps to express confidence.

4. No.
    - It says I know where I'm going.
    - It shows the strength of your leadership.
    - No to anything random and distracting.
    - No helps express conviction.
    - It doesn't have to be a harsh word if said kindly.

5. I love you.
    - I know what that means.
    - I know what I'm doing when I say I love you.

6. **I appreciate you.**
   - **It is different from thank you.**
   - **It says I acknowledge you and I value you.**

7. **I am sorry.**
   - **I am sorry about what happened, whether it was my fault or not.**
   - **It says I understand that it matters. It expresses responsibility.**

8. **Count me in!**
   - **It means no pressure required.**
   - **It expresses that I am committed and reliable.**
   - **It expresses 'yes' and 'amen'.**

9. **Whatever it takes.**
   - **I don't mind what I do.**
   - **It expresses a right attitude.**
   - **It will take you wherever you want to go.**

10. **No worries!**
    - **It says I refuse to get my knickers twisted.**
    - **It helps to express resilience.**

"Careful words make for a careful life; careless talk may ruin everything. "

[Proverbs 13:3 The Message]

101

Words to Remember

1. MORE JESUS!
2. To know is to love.
3. My freedom is my problem.
4. Jump on the grace train; it's always moving forward.
5. Margin.
6. Simple Life.
7. Body & Soul.
8. You can never out-give God.
9. Never give up on people.
10. Romans 12 yourself.
11. There is no such thing as "sower's remorse".
12. Faithfulness is proven in the absence of the master.
13. Confide in haste, regret at leisure.
14. If the enemy knows you live by your feelings, he will feed you everything you feel like.
15. Honor begins and ends at home.
16. Spiritual maturity isn't based on how long you've known God, but on how long you've obeyed Him.
17. Bible says.
18. Eternity.
19. Breakfast Club.
20. Let's lead with our lives.

www.ingramcontent.com/pod-product-compliance
Lightning Source LLC
Chambersburg PA
CBHW072013150426
43194CB00008B/1088

* 9 7 8 0 9 8 4 0 3 8 7 1 8 *